PLANTS THAT CHANGED OUR LIVES

Martyn Baguley

Lismore Publications.

ISBN-13: 9798736848386
ISBN-10: 1477123456

Cover design by: Art Painter
Library of Congress Control Number: 2018675309
Printed in the United States of America

Photographs courtesy of Pixabay

CONTENTS

INTRODUCTION

In his book 'Seeds of Change', Henry Hobhouse relates stories about 'Five plants that transformed mankind', namely quinine, sugar, tea, cotton and the potato. The book came to my mind in 2017 when I was asked to write a monthly series of articles about plants for several magazines. The more I read and thought about the subject the more intrigued I became about the influence that plants have had on mankind's history.

I thought that Hobhouse's book would be a good source of information about five plants, but it presented a challenge. Magazine editors mostly want feature articles to be limited to 800 to 1000 words: Hobhouse wrote an average of 22000 words about each plant! Incorporating all of his fascinating facts into maximum 1000 word articles would be a major précising challenge. Furthermore, I never rely on one source of information for my articles, so the more my researches discovered about the plants the greater the challenge would be.

And that wasn't the entire problem. The prospect was for the series of articles to run for more than five months - in fact it eventually continued for two years and only ended when a new editor asked me to come up with another plant subject (See 'Books by the author' - 'Plant Intelligence, Fact or Fiction?'). What other plants have significantly influenced our history? Where would all the information come from?

It was an interesting and rewarding challenge for someone who is fascinated by plants. For three years during my student days I had spent countless days in the university's botany department lecture theatre and laboratory studying plant anatomy, ecology, pathology, physiology and other long-forgotten subjects, but nothing about the influence plants had been on our history. Now, in my dotage, the opportunity had come to research the subject.

During a working visit to Ghana, I went into one of the few remaining areas of native tropical forest. Standing by a huge, ancient tree I noticed that the bottom of the trunk had been hacked at, presumably by an axe. I asked my Ghanaian forester host why this had been done. 'For medicine', he said. 'What sort of medicine?' I asked. 'For the internal rash caused by measles', he said without hesitation. As we walked further into the forest I noticed that the bark of many other different species of trees had similarly been attacked by axes. My host could tell me exactly what the medicine made from the bark of every tree was used for. Then he suddenly stopped and said, 'But ask two people what the bark of any tree is useful for and you will get two different answers'.
That experience came to my mind as I began to think about which plants I should include in my series of articles. The more research I did the more I came to think that there is a story to tell about every plant. That's an exaggeration, but there are fascinating stories to tell about the way many plants have influenced the lives of our ancestors, from the earliest hominids, and continue to influence our lives today.

What follows in this book is a compilation of the articles about twenty one plants, distilled from information gleaned from many sources and first published in magazines in the United Kingdom and Republic of Ireland between 2017 and 2019. I hope that my enthusiasm for the subject shines through my scribbles and they will enthuse at least some of my readers. Maybe you will be one of them.

Martyn Baguley

WILD CABBAGE

A hundred years ago in the wastes of Labrador in northern Canada, a thirty-year old fur trapper could have been seen during the bitterly freezing winter months filling large wooden barrels with alternating layers of sea water and cabbage leaves. Because his wife desperately missed having fresh vegetables during the winter, having noticed the native Inuit's way of fast freezing fish he had applied their methods to cabbage and discovered that if fast frozen, when thawed the leaves tasted exactly like fresh cabbage. Freezing food wasn't new, but much frozen food tasted mushy when thawed: the fur trapper had discovered that instant freezing was the answer. I'm sure you will recognize his name - Clarence Birdseye. He went on to make a fortune out of his idea.

The cabbage leaves he used in his early freezing experiments had travelled a long way through history. For thousands of years they had been evolving from the wild cabbage, *Brassica oleracea*, (*Brassica* the Latin word for a cabbage: *oleracea* meaning suitable for cooking).

If Darwin's concept of 'Evolution by Natural Selection' hadn't produced wild cabbage in the past – or to be precise wild cabbages as there are many different sub-species - we would never have come to know broccoli, Brussels sprouts, cauliflower, kale, oilseed rape (you can probably think of many other so-called 'greens'). Wild cabbage is a polymorphic plant, which is a posh way of saying that it can evolve into many different forms. Grow any mix of these together and in time they will revert to their wild cabbage ancestor. Although native to Europe and west Asia no-one knows where they first appeared. In Britain it was first recorded in 1548 growing on the White Cliffs of Dover. Relatively short-lived (some 20 years) and now classified as a nationally scarce plant, it is mainly found in the south of England and Wales on limestone or chalk maritime cliffs in mixed grassland communities.

There are records of cabbage being cultivated in China since 4000BC. It was probably first domesticated in Europe 3000 years ago from wild plants that had thick leaves which can retain water and survive in cold regions where water was scarce. Our ancestors would have selected plants with the biggest leaves and used their seeds for the next generation. By 500BC kale-like plants had been developed. During the first century AD artificial selection of kale with tightly bunched leaves probably eventually produced plants similar to the ball-headed cabbages we know today

The Greeks knew cabbage at least as early as the fourth century BC. The Greek philosopher Diogenes (412-323 BC) is said to have lived entirely on cabbage and water (he must have been a very lonely philosopher). The Emperor Claudius (10-54AD) asked the Roman Senate to vote on whether there was any dish better than corned beef and cabbage. Unsurprisingly the senators voted 'nay'. Pliny the Elder (23-79AD), in his book *Natural History*, called it 'the most highly esteemed of all the garden vegetables'. The Romans gave us the word 'vegetable', derived from the Latin *vegere* which means to animate or enliven.

Celtic people, who began occupying Britain from Western Europe some five hundred years before the Romans invaded in 55BC, may have brought wild cabbage plants with them. The name 'cabbage' probably derives from the Celtic name *kad* or *kap* via the Middle French word for the vegetable, *cabus*.

The Cure-all Cabbage

With such a long relationship with mankind it isn't surprising that cabbage established a place in medical lore that persists to this day. Scrolls dating back to 1000BC mention white cabbage as a cure for baldness. Pliny claimed that for six hundred years his fellow Romans hadn't needed doctors because they had cured everything with cabbages. For centuries scurvy was a serious winter illness that our ancestors cured by eating cabbage and 'sauerkraut' (pickled cabbage) which contains more vitamin C than oranges. Captain Cook took sixty kegs of sauerkraut on his voyages of exploration: none of his crews died from scurvy because he flogged anyone who didn't eat some. That begs the question – would he have reached, charted and claimed the east coast of Australia for Great Britain without cabbages?

With such a reputation it isn't surprising that cabbage was a popular winter food and an essential part of Christmas and New Year meals for our ancestors. Belief in its benefits has persisted to the present. A heated cabbage leaf placed on a septic wound is believed to be effective in drawing out the infection (Shetland 1994). A cabbage leaf wrapped round a swollen knee can reduce the swelling (Cambridge 1963): a hangover can be cured by drinking cabbage water (Devon 1991) - a mixture of cabbage water and vinegar is believed by some today to be a good treatment for a hangover: fresh cabbage leaves can be used to treat ulcers (Ireland 1965): chewing cabbage leaves can relieve headaches (Devon 1991).

Many breastfeeding women have called on the ancient tradition of putting cabbage leaves in their bras (should I have said 'brassieres'?) to get relief from mastitis, which - for the benefit of unworldly male readers - causes breast tissue to become sore and inflamed. Fanciful? Seemingly not. In a paper published in January 2019, Dr. Rajni Sharma says 'The current available evidence suggests that cabbage leaf treatment helps reduce pain in breast engorgement and lengthens breastfeeding duration'. He recommends that it 'should be promoted -- as a routine care for all postnatal mothers having breast engorgement for reducing pain'. There is a good scientific reason. Cabbages contain glucosinolates, chemical actions on which convert them to mustard oil that has long been used as a home remedy for swelling.

The Country Lore Cabbage

Our innately superstitious ancestors relied heavily on omens to help them with all the uncertainties of life. Love divination was especially important to them and for this purpose cabbages, together with many other objects, played a part. A verse often written on Valentine Day cards went:

> *My love is like a cabbage*
> *Often cut in two*
> *The leaves I give to others*
> *The heart I give to you*

At Halloween blindfolded girls were sent out in pairs to pull up the first cabbage they could find. If it came up with a lot of soil attached they would become wealthy; if not they would be poor. How the cabbage leaves tasted determined the future spouse's disposition - sweet or sour. Cabbage stalks determined the characteristics of future spouses, straight, crooked, long or short. A plant with club root foretold potential physical infirmities.

Possibly because it is mentioned in Robert Burn's 1787 poem 'Halloween', some references to superstitions associated with cabbages suggest that they were exclusively Irish and Scottish, but they also crop up (no pun intended) in county-related traditions in England. Details vary but practices are essentially similar to one recorded in Hertfordshire in 1912 viz. 'If a girl go into the garden and cut a cabbage as the clock strikes twelve, the wraith of her future husband will then appear'

For countless generations of our ancestors cabbages have been associated with their wellbeing and love lives, so it's nice that the plant is recognized on World Cabbage Day. It's on February 17th – appropriately only three days after Valentine's Day.

Four Of The Best Known 'Cultivars' Of Wild Cabbage

Cabbage: probably the first cultivar to be domesticated. The earliest record of the round-headed cabbages we use today is in the 14th century when they are mentioned in manuscripts and said to be popular with all classes of people.

Cauliflower: believed to have originated in Cyprus, the Roman 1st century writer Pliny called it 'cyma' and said 'Of all the varieties of cabbage the most pleasant-tasted is cyma'. Well known in Europe by the Middle Ages it was first mentioned by the English herbalist John Gerard in his 1597 *'Herbal'* where he recommended that it should be sown on a hot dung pile in spring. The name derives from the Italian *caoli fiori* meaning 'cabbage flower'.

Brussels Sprouts: the much-quoted statement that it was first discovered in Brussels in 1750 is doubted as it was being cultivated in Europe in the 16th century. There is a possible scientific explanation why some people, especially children, dislike it. .We share a gene with our Neanderthal ancestors that makes a proportion of the population dislike a chemical that give sprouts their bitter taste. A pity because the nutritional value of sprouts is legendary.

Broccoli: grown for its edible flower buds and stalk it was cultivated in Italy in early Roman times and introduced into England in the mid 1800s when it was called 'Italian asparagus'. The name derives from the Italian word *broccolo,* which means "the flowering crest of a cabbage,"

THE FOXGLOVE

The year is 1775. Accompanied by a local doctor, thirty four year old Dr.William Withering is travelling in a dog cart along lanes near Stafford when his companion asks him if he would mind if they interrupted their journey by calling at a cottage they were passing to see one of his poor elderly patients who is suffering from a heart condition and dropsy. Withering agrees and offers to provide a second medical opinion, which his companion readily accepts. The woman is in an upstairs bedroom, very poorly and the two doctors agree that there is nothing they can do for her. They go downstairs and tell the small assembly of relatives and friends to prepare for the worst. (Don't despair – this true story has a happy ending).

A few weeks later fortune decreed that Dr.Withering found himself passing the same cottage. Deciding to enquire about the woman's condition he was surprised when she answered the door and appeared in excellent health. She told him that a gypsy woman had called at the cottage and when told what her ailments were went away and returned with a selection of herbs from which she made an infusion. After taking several doses the patient's heart beat had become normal and her health had recovered. Withering spent months tracking down the gipsy and when he found her he managed to persuade her to show him all the herbs that she used to make the infusion. The principal ingredient was leaves of the foxglove *Digitals purpurea.*

The foxglove plant had been known to have medicinal properties as far back as the 13th century. The German physician Leonhard Fuchs (1501-1566) recommended it for 'the scattering of dropsy', the old term used to describe swelling of soft tissues due to the accumulation of excess water in the body. Fuchs first used the word *digitalis* because he thought that the flower resembled a 'fingerhut', the German word for a fingerstall, *digitus* being the Latin for a finger. In his book *Herball, or Generall Historie of Plantes*, the respected Elizabethan herbalist and botanist John Gerard (1545 to 1612) recommended an expectorant made by boiling foxglove in water or wine to relieve *'thick toughnesse of grosse and slimie flegme and naughty humours'.* Culpepper (1616 to 1654) inherited Gerard's faith in the plant. In his Complete Herbal he described it as *'being of a gentle cleansing nature, and withal very friendly to nature'. He recommended a decoction made of foxglove mixed with 'four ounces of Polipody (fern) in ale' as a cure for falling sickness (epilepsy).*

But the use of foxglove as medicaments was hit and miss, shrouded in folklore and superstition and associated with the belief in fairies. Juice or dew collected from the plant was used in rituals to commune with them and the leaves were believed to help break fairy spells. Foxgloves were planted to invite fairies to visit and foxglove flowers were carried around to attract fairy energy.

Because herbalists didn't know how digitalis worked foxglove was accredited with being useful for countless medical conditions. Foxglove tea, an infusion of the leaves, was taken for colds, fevers and catarrh, and compresses were used for the treatment of ulcers, swellings and bruises. In Dr. Richard Neale's book published in 1877, '*Neale's Medical Digest*', it was recommended for the treatment of 32 conditions including bronchitis, tuberculosis and typhoid. That may have persuaded the artist Van Gogh to try it to cure his epilepsy.

By carrying out long-term experiments on 163 patients suffering from dropsy, keeping detailed scientific records and publishing his results in *'An Account of the Foxglove and Some of its Medicinal Uses'* in 1785, Withering started what was to become foxglove's ultimate destiny as the source of the drug digitalis. It took a long time before the plant's healing powers were fully understood and harnessed but countless numbers of people suffering from heart disease owe it their lives.

Bloody Bells, Bloody Man's Fingers, Deadman's Bells and many more sinister names bespeak foxglove's association with pagan superstition and magic. With the coming of Christianity to Britain it was removed from these sinister associations by being given more benign names like Lady's Gloves and Virgin's Fingers. One ancient belief was that the flowers were bewitched by fairies, hobgoblins and elves who fitted them over the paws of foxes so that they could creep silently up to poultry. That belief may account for the Anglo-Saxon name for the plant being *foxes glofa* or *foxes-clife*, hence today's name of foxglove.

I can think of no better words to summarize the profound effect that the foxglove has had on our lives than those I found in the old saying - 'It can raise the dead and it can kill the living'.

INCENSE TREES

Boswellia sacra incense

In 1857 the ever-popular carol 'We Three Kings' was written by the Reverend John Henry Hopkins for the General Theological Seminary in New York City as part of their Christmas pageant.

For years, when I was a child, I thought that the three 'Kings' who brought gifts to the baby Jesus came from Orientar - the first line of the carol definitely says 'We three kings of Orientar'. If that wasn't confusing enough for young minds, most of us probably first heard of, and were confused by, the words 'frankincense' and 'myrrh' which feature in the carol. The Rev. Hopkins wasn't very helpful - all he told us was that frankincense owned 'a Deity nigh' and myrrh 'breathes a life of gathering gloom' I will try now to throw some light on the 'gathering gloom'.

Frankincense is an aromatic resin obtained from four species of trees of the *Boswellia* genus, particularly *B. sacra* ('Boswellia' don't ask me why it is attributed to the 18C James Boswell a friend of Dr. Johnson; '*sacra*' from the Latin word *sacrum,* a sacred thing). The trees are native to Oman, Somalia and Yemen. Growing up to a height of eight metres in dry, rocky areas, they are normally multi-stemmed and look a bit like a cross between a crab apple and a hawthorn. The English botanist William Botting (1843-1924) was less flattering: he described them as looking like 'a decomposing animal'. Resins are obtained from the trees by scoring the bark two or three times a year in light horizontal lines from which a gummy sap oozes. When the sap droplets have dried they are scraped off and allowed to harden. After a few years the trees are left to rest before the process is started again. Each Boswellia species gives rise to a different type of resin. The purest and most expensive comes from *B.sacra*.

The word *frankincense* derives from the Old French *franc encens* which means high-quality incense. When burnt it produces a psycho-active substance called trahydrocannabinole, a crystalline compound that is the main active ingredient of cannabis. This expands consciousness and increases awareness of the spiritual world, which would explain why it has been used for thousands of years in religious ceremonies. The earliest record of it being used was found on the 15th century BC tomb of the Egyptian Queen Hatshepsut. Trade in frankincense peaked during the time of the Roman Empire: the Emperor Nero is said to have burned tons of it during ceremonies.

There were other practical reasons for its use. With temples being effectively giant slaughterhouses due to blood sacrifices being carried out in them, incense was needed to mask the foul smells. Before the advent of soap and daily bathing, the sweet smoke that comes from burning frankincense was used by people to make themselves smell better and Egyptian women ground the charred resin into a powder called kohl which they used to make the black eyeliner, distinctive of many figures in Egyptian art.

There is concern about Boswellia tree populations which some say are declining due to browsing by herbivores, attacks by a longhorn beetle and over-exploitation. From recent research some 80% of seeds produced by trees which have not been tapped for resin germinate, but only 16% germinate from trees which are heavily tapped.

Myrrh is also a resin obtained from thorny bushes or small trees of the *Commifora* genus, particularly *C.myrrh* ('*Commiphora* derived from the Greek word *kommi* meaning gum, '*myrrh*' originally from the Hebrew *murr* meaning bitter). The genus is native to the eastern Mediterranean, Ethiopia, the Arabian Peninsula and Somalia. The gum, which is harvested in the same way as frankincense, coagulates, quickly becoming hard and glossy and darkening in colour with time. Like frankincense, myrrh has been used for millennia in incense, perfumes and holy ointments. Ancient Egyptians used it in embalming mixtures and burnt pellets of the resin to deter fleas. Mixed with wine it was offered to prisoners prior to execution to ease pain: it was the only small kindness offered to Jesus prior to his crucifixion (Mark ch15v23)

The medicinal qualities of both frankincense and myrrh were well known to our ancestors who, wisely or not, used them to treat wounds, cure hemlock poisoning, leprosy, snakebites, diarrhoea, plague, scurvy and even baldness. They are used today in wide-ranging medicaments and cosmetics.

The scrubby trees may have even more to give to mankind. In 2008, working on mice, researchers at the Hebrew University in Jerusalem said that evidence indicates that the aroma of frankincense might help to reduce anxiety and depression. The active ingredient is said to use different mechanisms than that of traditional drugs so frankincense may offer the potential to develop anti-depressants and anxiety-suppressing drugs which are free of undesirable side effects.

The research is still in progress, or perhaps I should say it is -

'Westward leading, still proceeding'.

THE BITTER VETCH

I had no idea how much my eating of 9000 peas a year – a figure quoted in the British Edible Pulses Association's website as the consumption of an average person - was doing to combat climate change and improve my health. Apparently British pea growers are helping to reduce greenhouse gas emissions and producing a food which lowers cholesterol, is low in fat, gluten free, rich in minerals and, compared with other things we eat, requires relatively little water. With (in 2017) some 700 farmers in Britain producing 90% of our annual consumption of peas on 35000 hectares (equivalent to 7000 football pitches), peas are big business. And it is all thanks to species of vetch, commonly called wild peas, the remote ancestors of the peas we eat today, the seeds of *Pisum sativum;* '*Pisum* the Latin word for a pea, *sativa* meaning cultivated.

The bitter vetch, *Vicia ervilia* ('*Vicia*' is the Latin for a vetch; *ervum* the Latin name for bitter vetch: so that must make it a bitter vetch vetch) is thought to have been one of the first domesticated crops. From archaeological research it was grown in the near east by our Neolithic ancestors 12,000 years ago. The seeds, which contain compounds related to cyanide so are potentially poisonous, are lentil-like and very bitter. To make them edible they would have had to be boiled in many changes of water to leach out the bitterness and toxicity. Constant selection improved the yield and by the 3rd century BC they must have started to be cultivated because the peripatetic Greek philosopher Theophrastus mentions peas as being sown late in winter because of their tenderness.

Field or wild peas are mentioned as helping to combat famine for our ancestors during the Middle Ages. The distinction between field and garden peas dates from the early 1600s but it wasn't until late in the 17th century that Europeans started what came to be a fashionable practice of eating fresh peas, then considered to be a delicacy. Being nutritious and easy to store on ships, dried peas were one of the essential foods taken by people preparing to sail to the American colonies during the 17th century and they were the first crops planted by colonists on arrival. Louis XIV of France was first introduced to green peas in January 1660 when, with a staged fanfare, he was presented with a hamper of them. After being shelled by a notable of the French Court the peas were ceremoniously presented to the King and Queen in small dishes.

Thanks to a monk we owe a lot to *Pisum sativum.* Johann Gregor Mendel (1822-1884) was the son of poor peasant farmers in what is now the Czech Republic. When aged twenty-one, dictated, on his own admission, more by circumstances than religious conviction, he entered an Augustinian Monastery in Brno. It was a fortunate choice: in the monastery he became part of a cultural and scientific circle and was encouraged to continue his education, spending three years at the University of Vienna where he studied physics, chemistry and zoology. In 1856 he began a ten year study of patterns of inheritance. His first choice of subject for the study, mice, was stopped because his bishop didn't like a priest conducting experiments that involved sex. Settling on garden peas he cultivated some 29,000 plants in order to study the inheritance of seven characteristics including height, flower colour, seed colour and seed shape. His experiments, the results of which he published in a paper which he read to the Natural History Society of Brno in 1865, were the foundation of what are known today as Mendel's Laws of Inheritance.

What we now call a pea first appeared in Old English, the language of the Anglo-Saxons, as *pise.* That evolved into *pease* (plural *peason)* as in pease pudding. With the passage of time *pease* came to mean the plural, so the 's' and '*e*' were dropped and a single pea became a '*pea*'.

With such a long relationship with Homo sapiens it's not surprising that pea folklore developed. Farmers believed that it would be a good year for peas if hedges dripped on Valentine's morning (Cambridgeshire 1952). If a pod containing nine peas was put over a door the first person to enter was believed to have the name or initial of a future lover (Ireland 1908). An old European remedy for getting rid of warts was (is?) to wrap a pea in paper and bury it saying 'As this pea shall rot away warts will soon decay'.

Last, but by no means least, there is a pea-eating etiquette. Tempting though it may be to shovel them up, the polite way to eat them is to squash them on the back of a fork. Not a lot of people know that.

COFFEE

Imagine for a moment that the year is 1735 and you are in the German City of Leipzig. (You haven't been to Leipzig? I did say 'imagine'). As you stroll along *Cather Strasse* Bach-like orchestral music comes from a cafe. The music fades, replaced by an angry tuneless baritone voice -

'You wicked child, you disobedient girl! When will I get my way; give up coffee!'

The music is 'Bach-like' because it is his. The words were by the poet and librettist Christian Henrici. You are near Zimmerman's Coffee House and listening to Johann Sebastian Bach's Coffee Cantata which he and Henrici wrote for The Collegium Musicum, a small musical group based there. It was the nearest Bach ever got to writing music for an opera.

Bach loved his coffee, as did most of the fashionable and literary set in the 18th century. Its popularity had started earlier – much earlier. Travellers, including Marco Polo, are credited with bringing coffee to Europe from the Near East in the 17th century. Like most new things, especially anything coming from the Orient, initially it was treated with suspicion. When it first arrived in Venice in 1615 the clergy condemned it as being the 'bitter invention of Satan'. Opposition to it was so intense that Pope Clement VIII was asked to adjudicate. After sampling a mug of Java coffee he said 'This devil's drink is delicious. We should cheat the devil by baptizing it'.

Although opposition persisted, with papal endorsement there was no stopping its growth in popularity. Coffee houses, which also served tea and chocolate, spread throughout Europe, becoming social centres where the great and good met to debate commerce, politics and general affairs of the day. In England the name 'penny universities' was coined for them, because for the price of a one penny cup of coffee men could engage in stimulating and educational conversation. Women generally weren't barred from them but they were considered to be unsuitable places for a 'lady' who wanted to preserve her respectability. By the mid-17th century there were some three hundred coffee houses in London alone: such reputable institutions as Lloyds of London, The Royal Society and Tatler Magazine can all trace their roots to London coffee houses.

It wasn't to last. For many long-debated reasons the coffee houses' popularity, status and authority began to decline during the second half of the 18th century and by 1900, having become objects of ridicule, they had almost completely disappeared in England. But they are back now with a vengeance: the only difference being that 17th century huddles of male intelligentsia have been replaced by 21st century loners with laptops.

For all this history we have to thank an unimpressive shrub which is native to what we now call Ethiopia, and Kaldi, a ninth century goatherd. The legend goes that Kaldi, searching for his lost herd of goats, found them acting erratically after eating red fruits growing on shrubs which, in 1753, Linnaeus classified as *Coffea arabica.* With his curiosity aroused he ate some himself and found that they made him hyperactive. He took some of the fruits to a monastery where the monks threw them onto a fire to destroy them, but the pleasant aroma persuaded them to give them a second chance. They put roasted beans into mugs of hot water and the drink of coffee was born.

It's a nice story but probably apocryphal as there are records of coffee beans being chewed as a stimulant centuries before Kaldi's alleged discovery. People would mix ground up coffee beans with butter and animal fat to eat on long journeys and Sudanese slaves would chew them to help them to survive. Coffee shrubs started to be cultivated during the 14th century in Arabic countries, from which it spread throughout Egypt, Syria and Turkey. In ancient Arab countries coffee was considered to be such an essential part of everyday life that a wife could win a claim for marital separation if her husband refused to produce coffee for her.

The name 'coffee' evolved from the Italian *caffee* which came from the Turkish *kahveh* and Arabic *gahwah.* There are about a hundred species of the *Coffea* genus but only two, *C.arabica* and *C. canephora*, are economically important: some 60 to 70% of the coffee we drink comes from varieties of *C.arabica* alone. Coffee plants are woody shrubs or small trees which, in their natural environment, grow up to a height of four metres and live for about seventy years. When some three years old they begin to produce white, highly scented flowers which take nine months to develop into fruits called 'cherries' which enclose two seeds, which we call 'beans'. Unusually for plants, fruit ripening is what botanists call 'asynchronous', which is the posh way of saying that at any one time during the fruiting period variable percentage mixes of ripe (red), green and dry cherries can be found growing together on the same branch. The reason is not fully understood: one academic paper suggests that it might be due to the occurrence of sporadic light rains during the latter phases of flower bud development being responsible for plants having several blossom periods.

Coffee's claimed benefits are numerous. Regular coffee drinkers are said to have one third fewer asthma symptoms; some scientists say that coffee protects the liver and may lower the risks of developing type 2 diabetes, dementia and Parkinson's disease; coffee drinkers may have a lower risk of developing some cancers. Even coffee's aroma is now being said to have hitherto unappreciated benefits. During 2008 researchers in Seoul National University found that the smell of coffee beans affected gene and protein activity in the brains of rats, some of which are linked to stress relief. So even if you don't like the taste of coffee perhaps a coffee fragrance room spray or diffuser will give you a morning lift.

THE CACAO TREE

On 15th August 1502, during his fourth visit to the 'New World', whilst exploring near an island off the coast of what is now called Honduras, Christopher Columbus encountered a native Mayan trader in a large canoe filled with a variety of goods including what the Spaniards thought looked like almonds (It's said that Columbus thought they were goats' excrement). In good conquistadorial fashion Columbus seized the canoe and took the contents on board his ship where the crew were puzzled by the importance the natives seemed to attach to the 'almonds'. Later Columbus' son Ferdinand wrote; *"They seemed to hold these almonds at a great price; for when they were brought on board ship together with their goods, I observed that when any of these almonds fell, they all stooped to pick them up, as if an eye had fallen."* The 'almonds' were cacoa beans, the seeds of cacao trees

Although Columbus is credited with bringing the first cacao beans back to Europe they were considered to be far less interesting than the other treasures on board his galleons. No-one could have guessed then that the humble beans would spawn a world-wide industry estimated to be worth some £40 billion today.

In 1753 the Swedish botanist Carl Linnaeus gave the cacao tree the botanical name *Theobroma cacao;* '*Theobroma*' from the Greek for 'food of the gods', '*cacao*' said to derive from the Aztec word '*xocolatl*', '*xococ*' meaning bitter, '*atl*' for water (You're not alone - I can't see the connection either). In its natural habitat it is a spindly, evergreen tree which is often found growing in clumps in the shade of giant tropical rain forest trees along river banks where the roots can be flooded for much of the year. Nothing particularly exceptional in that: but the cacao tree has an unusual botanical trait – it's cauliflorous. No, it has nothing to do with caulflowers; the word comes from the Latin words *caulis,* meaning stem, and *flor* meaning flower.

Unlike most woody plants that produce flowers and fruits on young leafy shoots, cauliflorous plants produce them on their main stems. Botanists debated why this characteristic, which is not uncommon among smaller trees in rainforests, has evolved. Then entomologists discovered that about 5% of the pretty, small, smell-free cacao tree flowers are pollinated mainly by tiny midges which only fly up to a height of about 6 metres above ground. So the tree sensibly (sorry – an anthropomorphism) makes sure its flowers grow where the midges will find them. And cauliflory provides another benefit. The small proportion of fertilized flowers grow into huge, multi-coloured fruits, called pods, up to 30cms long, 10cms wide and 500gms in weight. Ripening on the tree the pods contain 30 to 40 beans encased in white, juicy pulp. These are eagerly sought by small mammals and birds which pick them off the tree and carry them several metres away from the parent tree where they gorge on the fleshy pulp. They reject the bitter tasting seeds, so these are left to germinate in an ideal growing environment. I think that's clever.

The wild cacao trees to chocolate story is well documented, the subject of several books and far too long to summarize in a short article (You want more? Google will help, but look out for inconsistencies and contradictions). Suffice it to say here that the story goes back some 4000 years in Central America, where archaeologists have found the remains of ceramic vessels containing residues of cacao drinks dating back to 1900BC. Cacao trees aren't easy to cultivate; yields are low so inevitably cacao beans became an expensive commodity. As everyone wanted them they began to be used as a form of currency. That would have explained why the Mayans Columbus encountered attached such importance to the 'almonds'.

At the time of the Spanish conquests cacao bean currency was rated more highly than gold by the Aztec people who had seized much of the Mayan land. A cloth bag containing 8000 beans was a standard Aztec measure. There is a record of the Aztec empire being paid a yearly tribute of 980 loads of cacao beans, each load representing exactly 8000 beans (Counting 7.84 million beans to pay the annual tribute must have been an unenviable job). In 1545 a cloth cloak cost 80 to 100 beans, a good turkey or a slave could be exchanged for 100 beans and a ripe avocado or tomato for 1 bean. Predictably the use of beans as currency encouraged dishonesty and there are records of beans being debased by removing the stone and replacing it with dirt.

Cacao beans were the main barter currency of the Aztecs and of such importance that their value was officially fixed in 1555 by a decree which valued one Spanish real equivalent to 140 cacao beans. Their use as currency spread throughout central South America, persisted well into the 19th century and even as recently as the early 20th century some small tribes in Mexico and Central America would exchange 40 cacao beans for any small silver coin.

Only poorer quality cacao beans were used by the Aztecs as currency, but why did a bulky, perishable commodity like cacao beans become valued as currency at all? Probably because they were very highly valued by the Aztecs for making the bitter drink which was used for important ceremonial occasions. The history of cacao beans as a form of currency reminds us that anything that is widely accepted as having social significance can derive an exchange value.

So you can tell the next person who quotes the cliché 'money doesn't grow on trees' that once upon a time it did.

THE WILD HOP

A bove the end aisle in my local supermarket is a sign 'Ales and Beers'. The stock on the shelves is bewildering for the casual drinker: bottles of so-called 'Beers', with names like Blodwen's, Big Boy, Lord's and Grumpy Bastard are packed between India Pale, Amber and Blonde 'Ales' and unclassified bottles of 'Piddle In A Bottle' (yes, really), 'Skull Splitter' and 'Mendip Twister'. (Please note these are not personal recommendations). Beer/ale aficionado readers will know the difference between ales and beers (it has to do with the way they are made), but for most of us the words beer and ale are synonymous.

Beverages brewed from grain and flavoured with a wide variety of herbs, but not hops, are mankind's oldest manufactured drinks. It was a popular tipple in ancient Egypt and, called *zythos*, a daily drink of the Greeks in 700BC. It was the daily tipple for Julius Caesar's soldiers. As the Roman legions invaded Europe and eventually Britain the taste for barley brew travelled with them. The Saxons who settled in Britain after the Romans left were prodigious ale quaffers; the name 'ale' derives from the Anglo Saxon *ealu.* Using brewing methods learned from the Romans they sprouted then dried (malted) barley, flavoured it with spices and herbs like marjoram, ground ivy, broom, meadow sweet and bog myrtle, then boiled it and left it to ferment. The process made it relatively bug free and much safer as a daily drink than water.

The earliest records of hops being used for brewing in Britain are in 1412. Long before then brewers in Germany and Flanders had discovered the advantages the addition of hops brought to what was called *bier* or *beer,* particularly in extending its drinkable life. There is good evidence that hops were being grown commercially in North Germany in the 1200s to supply breweries in the Hansa towns from which beer was exported at least as early as the 13th century.

Surprisingly *biére,* as the English King Henry VI called it in the 1400s, was resisted by the ale-drinking English. There was resistance to adulterating good English 'ale' with 'foreign' hops. But hop-brewed beer was imported from abroad to quench the thirst of the many Dutch weavers who had settled in East Anglia and the southern counties to work in the wool-weaving industry.

The English brewers didn't have an easy time. There was considerable opposition against the use of hops for brewing and violent reactions by both ale brewers and drinkers against the use of them by beer brewers from the Low Countries. Between 1440 and 1540 various authorities forbade ale brewers, who remained distinct from beer brewers until at least the 17th century, from putting hops in their ale.

Who would have thought that a humble climbing hedgerow plant could have caused so much trouble?

The wild hop's botanical name is *Humulus lupulus* - '*Humulus*' the Latin name of the hop plant; '*lupulus*' from the Latin for a wolf (*lupus*), reflecting the mistaken belief that the plant strangles other plants by climbing over them. The English origin of the word *hop* is uncertain but it probably derives from the Anglo-Saxon word *hoppan* which means to climb.

The first written record of hops in Europe was in 768AD. Long before hop plants were cultivated wild hops were collected from sites in Europe called *Humlanariae* (probably derived from *humela,* the Old German word for hops), locations where they were abundant. Botanists don't all agree that hops are native British plants; some say that the plants which are growing today in hedges are the descendants of plants which have escaped from cultivation. But from soil pollen remains we know that hops were growing wild in Southern England in Neolithic times.

The wild hop does grow in Ireland but isn't a native Irish plant. During the 18th century large quantities of commercial varieties of hops were imported into Ireland from England. In 1752 alone some 500 tons were imported through Dublin alone.

Hops were valued by our ancestors for their perceived medicinal qualities probably long before it was used for brewing. In the 8th Century AD Arab physicians prescribed syrup made from hops for treating fevers. Culpeper (1514-1541) recommended a decoction of hops for jaundice, headaches, worms and bad complexions. The German botanist Adam Lonitzer (1528-1586) recommended an infusion of hops for driving out melancholy. Pillows stuffed with warm hops were once a common remedy for relieving toothache, earache and neuralgia and hop poultices were used to reduce inflammation and rheumatic pain.

Humulus lupulus is recorded as being widespread in England so it isn't very difficult to find in hedgerows. If you find a plant raise a metaphorical glass to it for few plants have had such a profound influence on our history.

THE STINGING NETTLE

The experience is engraved on my memory.

When I was about five years old, whilst playing in a field one sunny summer afternoon wearing nothing more than my skimpy swimming trunks, I fell headlong into clump of stinging nettles (sorry if that made you cringe). Stung from head to toe and howling, I was carried home by my older sister where my mother plastered me all over with calamine lotion. I can't recall how long it took for the pain to subside, but I do remember that for years after I had a nettle phobia.

The name 'nettle' may come from the Anglo Saxon word for a needle, *'noedl'*, referring to the tiny hairs on the stems and undersides of the leaves which, if touched, pierce skin and inject formic acid, histamine and other chemicals. The hairs are believed to have evolved as a survival mechanism to protect the plant from being browsed by herbivores. Female plants have more stinging hairs than male plants, which may be because females need more protection because they have to invest more energy into producing seeds than males need to produce pollen. We should be grateful that the stings of our common nettle are relatively weak: the stings of a nettle found in Java – common name appropriately 'Devil's leaf' - can last for up to a year, cause lockjaw and even death. The botanical name of the stinging nettle is *Urtica dioeca*, '*Urtica*' derived from the Latin word *urere*, to burn or sting; '*dioeca*' from Greek meaning 'of two houses' which tells us that flowers are either male or female.

You would think that our ancestors would have avoided such a vindictive plant: I know, a plant can't be 'vindictive' - but I bet the photographer who, whilst photographing Linnaeus's botanical collection, was stung by a 200-year old nettle plant thought it was.

Vindictive or not, our ancestors have been trying to find uses for nettles for more than two millennia. In a Bronze Age burial site on the island of Fyn in Denmark researchers found a bronze container in which were the bones of a man wrapped in fabric. Initial analysis suggested that the cloth was made of flax, a plant which was cultivated in the region at the time, but subsequent research showed that the c2800 year old fabric was made from nettles. But not nettles which had grown in Denmark. During 2012 Professor Karin Frei of the University of Copenhagen analysed the strontium isotope levels in the plant fibres. These showed that the fabric had probably come from as far away as south-west Austria. Contrary to previous ideas that with the advent of agriculture cultivated plants like flax replaced wild plants like nettles for textile production, during the Bronze Age both wild and cultivated plants were used concurrently in Central Europe. Nettle fabrics are rated as highly as silk, which would explain why.

Nettles have served mankind in many other ways. Ancient Egyptians used nettle infusions to relieve arthritis. Hippocrates (460-377B.C.) recommended sixty-one nettle remedies for a plethora of conditions including dog bites, nose bleeds, pleurisy, asthma and mouth sores. Up to the tenth century nettles were recommended to treat shingles and constipation and in his *Complete Herbal* Culpeper (1514 - 1541) lists nettles for treating many conditions including "bladder stones or gravel, worms in children, an antiseptic for wounds and skin infections, gout, sciatica, joint aches, and as an antidote to venomous stings from animals". Today herbalists still use nettles "to bring dormant energies into action".

Many cultures have practiced 'Urtification', a process of flogging the body with fresh nettle plants to treat conditions like lethargy, coma, paralysis and even cholera and typhus. Roman soldiers are said to have brought seeds of *Urtica pilulifera* with them when they invaded Britain so that they would have nettle plants to stimulate their blood circulation in the cold climate and revive tired legs after long marches.

I haven't even touched on the use of nettles to eat and make drinks, for making paper, rope and dyes. And I won't. Far simpler for me to direct any interested readers to a book by Piers Warren, '101 Uses for the Stinging Nettle'.

Finally some hopefully helpful advice. If you are troubled by nettles in your garden dig up all the roots – don't just cut them down. Scientists have found that if nettles are heavily damaged they will regrow leaves and stems with higher densities of stinging hairs. This is the result of a chemical process called methylation which doesn't affect the genes (genotype) but, by modifying the DNA, does influence the stinging hair density (phenotype). So the more you damage the plants the more virulent their stings will become.

Clever? I call it a vindictive sting in the tail.

THE PINEAPPLE

In the National Trust's Ham House in Surrey, there is an oil painting of John Rose, the Royal Gardener, presenting a pineapple to King Charles 11. The event is said to have taken place in 1675 and the pineapple one of the first to have been grown in England. 'Hogwash' says an anonymous (presumably one of our American cousins) writer of one of the many articles on 'pineapples' websites, who goes on to give lots of reasons why the picture isn't authentic (including the fact that King Charles is shown without a moustache and he didn't shave it off until 1677). Readers of my scribbles will, I hope, know that my overriding ambition is not to write 'hogwash', so this started me on some in-depth detective work to find the (hopefully) true story. It's a complicated one. If you are sitting comfortably I'll begin.

The plant that we now call a pineapple is native to Brazil and Paraguay and the first humans to domesticate it were probably the Tupi-Guarani people. They sound charming: short and stout, light skinned with long black hair they lived in the coastal areas of Brazil, wore no clothes, painted their legs and thighs black and their main pastime was fighting rival tribes and fattening up prisoners of war for their favourite dish – human flesh. They were the first native inhabitants of the region to be encountered by Portuguese explorers in the 16th century: the Portuguese sailor Pero Vaz dre Caminha thought the women were beautiful: probably not surprising after spending months at sea.

Pineapples are herbaceous perennial plants which grow to a height of about 1.5 metres. They have short, stocky stems, tough, waxy leaves and produce up to some 200 flowers which fuse together to form the familiar pineapple fruit. Wild pineapples, which the ancestors of the Tupi-Guarani people first discovered and can still be found in Brazil, bear little resemblance to the pineapples we know today. They are small (about the size of an apple), packed with seeds, stringy and very sour. With such credentials it is surprising that the natives thought that they could be useful for anything. But thankfully they did. Long before the arrival of the first Europeans they had become domesticated and spread throughout South and Central America, Mexico and the West Indies.

Enter on the scene Christopher Columbus on his second package holiday to the West Indies. Following a record breaking Atlantic crossing (three week economy class; his first had taken three months), on 4th November 1493 he and members of his crew found and landed on a stunningly beautiful tropical island. Honouring a promise he had made to the monks during a pilgrimage to the monastery of Santa Maria de Guadalupe in Spain, he named the island Guadeloupe (presumably he couldn't spell). Fortunately for Columbus the native men were away on a slave raid, which was lucky because, like their ancestors, the native Carib people were renown cannibals. So the Europeans were able to explore inland to see what they could plunder.

The island was a treasure trove of things that were new to the Europeans -including pineapples. The Caribs loved the fruit.

When they weren't using it to make copious quantities of sweet wine they pounded it into a thick paste which they seasoned with capsicum and eat with meat (presumably often human). Unbeknown to them they had discovered that pineapples are the only known source of bromelian, an enzyme that can tenderize meat by digesting protein, which is why today the fruit is served with gammon and ham dishes and often features in weight-loss diets.

Columbus' account of the journey are lost, but writing later, and referring to his father's log books, his son Ferdinand recorded the moment that the fruit was first seen by a European: *'They also saw - - - some fruit that looked like green pine cones but were much larger; these were filled with solid pulp, like melon, but were much sweeter in taste and smell'.* The seminal words are 'pine cones' and 'sweeter'. It is the first time that pineapples are recorded as looking like pine cones and sweet things were a luxury in Europe due to the high price of sugar: discovering a sweet-tasting plant offered the prospect of considerable financial reward. But first they had to give it a name. Disdaining the cannibals' name, *anãnã* (keep that in mind), they settled on the Spanish word for a pine cone – *piña de Indes* (pine cone of the Indians).

After visiting Guatemala, Columbus spent nearly two and a half years exploring the islands now known as Haiti, Cuba and Jamaica before returning to Spain with his ships loaded with spoils of the expedition, including several ripe pineapples intended as presents for Kink Ferdinand and Queen Isabella. After a turbulent voyage, on 11th June 1496 the small fleet was welcomed back in the Bay of Cadiz by a band and crowds of cheering people. As the weary sailors unloaded the treasures their hearts must have sunk when they saw that all but one of the pineapples had turned to pulp during the long journey.

Nursing the one good pineapple Columbus went immediately to the Spanish Court and gave it to their Majesties. It must have been a nerve-wracking moment for him: the reaction of the King and Queen would determine whether or not the fruit was a potential gold mine. The moment was later recorded by an Italian, Peter

Maryr, tutor to the royal princes, who was present at the occasion.

'The most invincible King Ferdinand relates that he has eaten another fruit brought from these countries' and he *'prefers it to all others'*.

'Prefers it to all others'! Columbus couldn't have asked for a better testimonial for the fruit. The words were quoted to death in subsequent accounts of the event. The pineapple had been launched on the European stage with a royal seal of approval which carried enormous weight at the time. It was destined to be called the King of Fruits.

Spain's King Ferdinand may have been the first European king to give pineapples royal approval but it was mainly the Portuguese who were responsible for its speedy world-wide colonization of many tropical countries. During the sixteenth and early seventeenth centuries Portuguese explorers were responsible for taking pineapples along the west and east coasts of Africa, Guinea, the west coast of India and even China. In all these places it flourished where the climate was sufficiently warm. It was valued both as a delicious fruit and for making wine, and the leaf fibre was used to make cloth which was said to be equal in quality to silk. Columbus's rejection of the native Guadeloupe people's name for the fruit, *anãnã* (meaning excellent fruit) and adoption of the name *piña de Indes* seems to have been forgotten during the 16th century: *'Anana'*, or variants of the word, *was* and still is in forty two countries, the name given to the fruit.

With such a delectable reputation the 'anana' was probably well known in England by the early 1500s. In 1613 the English cleric Samuel Purchas (1577-1626) wrote *'Ananas is reckoned one of the best. In taste like an Apricocke, in shew a farre off like an Artichoke, but without prickles, very sweet of sent'*. Writing in 1624 The English explorer Captain John Smith (1580 – 1631), influenced by the resemblance of the fruit to a pine cone and the tradition of calling a new fruit an apple (and presumably unaware of the ananas name), was possibly the first person to call the fruit a pineapple.

No-one knows who first brought pineapples to England. The earliest record is in the diary of John Evelyn (1620 - 1706), horticulturalist friend of King Charles II, who said that the first fruits were given as a present to Oliver Cromwell in 1657. With the fruit's association with kings (the French priest Father du Tertre is credited with first calling it 'the King of Fruits') and Catholicism, it is not surprising that Cromwell, the quintessential puritan, didn't endorse it. Not so King Charles II – he loved it; particularly the symbolism of the 'crown' of leaves. In a public relations exercise par excellence, in 1668 he launched the fruit on the English scene at a dinner in honour of the French ambassador where, in accordance with tradition, the meal culminated in a tableau of extravagant desert courses all surrounding a pineapple balanced on an elevated silver salver. It was a fruitful way of advertising England's success as a colonizing power.

In the 17th century pineapples which had survived the journey from the West Indies could be ripened in England, but they couldn't be grown there. To propagate a pineapple from a crown or suckers to a ripe fruit required a constant noxious-fume-free air temperature of at least 60°F, a soil temperature of not less than 70°F and plenty of light and water, all beyond then current gardening technology. But King Charles, by establishing the pineapple as a status symbol, had started a pineapple mania. The English landowning gentry had to find a way of growing the fruit in England's distinctly non-tropical climate.

It wasn't going to be easy. Europe's first greenhouses were unheated and, with glass only on the south side, designed to protect oranges and lemon trees from frosts during the coldest months of the year. Pineapples needed controlled heat and light all year round. To add to the problems reliable thermometers weren't invented until 1714.

Encouraged by their employers and jealous of the success which Dutch gardeners, said to be the best in the world, had made growing pineapples, during the latter part of the 17th century English gardeners strove, often unsuccessfully, to grow the fruit.

But it wasn't until about 1714 that, after years of experimentation, Henry Telende, gardener for Sir Richard Decker at Richmond Green in West London, discovered a reliable way to grow consistently high quality pineapples. His secret was tanner's oak bark, obtained from leather working, mixed with horse manure to heat his hothouses. During July or August, pineapple crowns or suckers were planted in 6 inch pots which were plunged into hotbeds filled with equal amounts of tanners bark and horse manure. This resulted in a fermentation process that kept the plants warm. It all sounds simple, but it was far from that. Success depended on skilful monitoring to maintain hotbed temperatures between 25° C and 30°C for up to three months, the correct amount of watering and countless hours of TLC.

Inevitably Telende's success spread. In his book published in 1726 *'General Treatise of Husbandry and Gardening'*, the botanist Richard Bradley wrote, *'The fruit of the Ananas is soft, tender and delicate and exceeds all the Fruits of the World in Flavour and Richness of Taste'*. He went on to detail Telende's methods of cultivation. This alone must have inspired gentry throughout the British Isles to try to grow pineapples in their estate gardens (yes, 'British Isles': they were being grown on James Justice's estate near Edinburgh in 1728 and by Daniel Bullen in his nursery on Dublin's New Street from 1730). Interest in the fruit grew into a full-blown pineapple mania: the list of the landed gentry who were caught up in the craze reads like a Who's Who of Georgian Society. The costs were astronomical – some £80 (c£11000 today) to produce one edible fruit – so it's hardly surprising that pineapples grown on country estates were seldom eaten: they were mostly used as the poshest of all ornaments on Georgian dinner tables

Pineapple growing continued to be identified with a gentleman's wealth and their gardener's artistry well into the beginning of the 20th century: 'artistry' because before the advent of hot water heating systems for greenhouses in 1816 it was seen as being as much an art as a science.

It couldn't last. Following the failure of the orange crop due to disease, in 1864 large scale pineapple cultivation began in the Azores. An article in the *Journal of Horticulture* in 1872 said it all: *'the once-aristocratic figures on the costermonger's (fruit) barrow, and is retailed at the lowest figure imaginable'*.

After more than 100 years of being the epitome of gardening excellence the prestige of the King of Fruits met its nadir when it began to feature in a recipe for pineapple fritters in *Mrs Beeton's Book of Household Management*.

SUGAR CANE

Linnaeus gave sugarcane the botanical name *Saccharum officinarum:* '*Saccharum*' the Latin word for the reed-like plant; '*officinarum*' meaning of practical use to man. What an innocuous name to give to a plant which has been dubbed 'white death' and ranked with cocaine, alcohol and tobacco as causing serious ill health to generations of our ancestors.

Life today without sugar is inconceivable, yet for thousands of years civilizations before our own managed perfectly well without it. Most had some sorts of sweetening commodity which they used sparingly - honey and sugars made from partially dehydrating the saps of palm and maple trees – but starting in the seventeenth century it was western Christian civilizations which made sugar into a cheap, daily commodity used by everyone in huge quantities and the basis for great industries. Today about 70% of the sugar we use comes from sugar cane: the remaining 30% is derived from sugar beet; but that's another story.

The debate about where species of sugarcane originated (there are at least five distinct species) has persisted for decades. Recent evidence from the DNA of plant remains suggests that *Saccharum officinarum* is native to South East Asia where, some 10,000 years ago, our ancestors found that the pith of the plant was sweet if sucked or chewed. This encouraged both the cultivation of the plant and, carried by canoeing seafarers, its spread around the Eastern Pacific and Indian Oceans. From evidence found on the banks of the River Ganges, in Northern India, some 2,500 years ago people began boiling cane juice then cooling it in flat bowls to make crystals which were easier to store and transport than sugar canes. They called the crystals *khandi,* from which the present day word *candy* was derived.

Cane sugar, the name given to the dried sap of *Saccharum officinarum,* is thought to have become known in Western Europe following the first Crusade (1096-9). For centuries it was valued as a rare and expensive spice and only used in very small quantities as a medicine, but by the sixteenth century it was being more widely used in wealthy households.

The earliest record of sugarcane being grown commercially in Western Europe was by the Portuguese during the latter part of the 15th century on the Atlantic island of Madeira. During the early 1500s the Portuguese began establishing sugarcane plantations in Brazil, which they had laid claim to in 1500. This was motivated more by necessity than economics. The prevailing principle at the time was that countries could only claim colony status of land they had actually occupied. Sugarcane had been grown commercially in the West Indies as early as 1506 (Christopher Columbus took plants to Hispaniola during his first trip in 1493), so extensive sugar plantations were seen by the Portuguese as an effective way to establish their occupancy of Brazil.

Where sugarcane plantations went, slavery followed: some 12.5 million human beings are estimated to have been transported from Africa to the Americas between 1501 and 1867 to work the plantations. And there was a knock-on effect. Slaves had to be paid for; copper, brass, tobacco, rum and guns were needed to purchase them from African slave traders. This need was met by expansion of industrial production in Britain which fuelled in turn the growth of our present-day banking and insurance businesses. The repercussions of the sugarcane industry have persisted almost to the present day. In 1833, under the Slavery Abolition Act, Britain borrowed £20 million to buy the freedom of slaves from slave owners. The money wasn't paid off until 2015.

By 1800 in the United Kingdom only the rich could afford sugar: in terms of its energy value it cost more than ten times the price of potatoes. Most of the sugar imported was grown and harvested in the Caribbean: some 'expert' calculated that before 1808, when the last slave was legally landed in the West Indies, the sugar trade had killed proportionately more people than the drug trade does today. Every spoonful of sugar was said to equate to six days of a slave's life.

Don't feel guilty; no slaves are involved with the sugar trade now. We are the sugar slaves – because most of us crave sweetness. We associate 'sweet' with nice things. We say that someone we like is a 'sweetie'; you may need to 'sweet talk' someone; you are lucky if you have a 'sweetheart'; a bribe or inducement is called a 'sweetener'; some-one who has an amiable disposition is called 'sweet-tempered'.

And sugar crops up (pardon the pun) in some old traditions. Traditional Jewish housewarming gifts include sugar, to ensure that the occupant's home is blessed with sweetness. Sugar-and-water days feature in English folklore when the custom was for children to visit wells on certain days of the year – often Easter or Palm Sunday – mix the water with some sugar and drink it. On Easter Sunday children would mix the spring water with a small quantity of sugar or honey, drink it and recite some doggerel. The origins of these traditions are obscure. They may be a relic of the belief that some wells are blessed with magical powers or be practical, the sugar masking an unpleasant water taste.

With such a dubious history sugarcane must surely be at the top of the league table of plants which have changed, and still are changing, peoples' lives.

THE NORWAY SPRUCE

In Britain in the 1960s, Christmas trees were predominantly five to eight year old Norway spruces (*Picea abies:* '*Picea*' the Latin name for the tree; '*abies*' the Latin name for a fir tree: so literally a spruce tree that looks like a fir). They were mostly bought during December from local shops or depots scattered around the countryside and cost around £1 a foot (equivalent to about £20 a foot today) with the grower having been paid for his years of loving care one shilling a foot (c£1 a foot today). They seldom had any roots but if they were freshly cut and you put the stumps into a bucket of water as soon as you got home, with a bit of luck they would keep their needles until Twelfth Night.

Not so if yours was one of the 25% of houses which had central heating in the 1960s; your lovely, ornament and tinsel-bedecked tree began to look more brown than green before Christmas and by Twelfth night your vacuum cleaner was clogged with green needles. How do I know all this? Trust me I was a forester at the time.

Central heating in houses grew rapidly in the 1970s - by 1980

60% of houses had central heating – and Picea abies became increasingly unpopular because the warmer the room the faster its needles fell. Foresters rose to the occasion firstly by offering pine trees which keep their needles better but frankly don't look much like a traditional Christmas tree, then 'designer' trees with exotic names; Nordmann, Fraser, Noble and Douglas firs, Serbian and blue spruce – all more expensive than Norway spruce. And that's where we are today. When you go to buy your next Christmas tree you will be faced with the dilemma of choosing a traditional, potential needle-shedding, Norway spruce or a wallet-busting designer tree with a name you probably will have difficulty remembering.

Queen Victoria and her consort Prince Albert are usually credited with starting the Christmas tree tradition in the United Kingdom when, in 1840 they imported several spruce trees from Germany. Although it is fair to say that this probably started the Christmas tree tradition, decorated spruces had been part of the Christmas tradition in Britain amongst the aristocracy long before then. Forty years earlier, during December 1800, Queen Charlotte, the German wife of George III, set up the first recorded tree at Queen's Lodge, Windsor. She must have been imbued with a German tradition that went back at least another two hundred years as there is a report dated 1605, from an unknown source, of how, at Yuletide people in Strasbourg '*Set up fir trees in the parlours and hang thereon cut out of many-coloured paper, apples, wafers, gold foil etc.*'

Far less well known is the fact that we owe a debt of gratitude to the Norway spruce for much more than being nice to look at during the festival of Christmas, for it has been largely responsible for the pleasure generations of people have derived from listening to music.

But first some botanical stuff.

Picea abies is native throughout Europe from Norway in the northwest, Poland in the east, the mountains of central Europe and south to the north of Greece. Between 1542 and 1546 the Italian, Andrea Amati, probably initially a lute maker (hence the name *'luthier'* which has persisted as the name for makers of violins, violas, cellos and guitars), made the first known violin. It only had three strings, but by 1555 he was making four stringed instruments much like a modern violin. The techniques he used have remained virtually unchanged for more than four hundred and fifty years. We will never know who, why or how, but some time before 1540 someone discovered that the best type of wood for making the top or 'table' of a violin came from Norway spruce trees growing at high elevations in the south of its natural range. Luthiers quickly discovered that although other species of wood used to make the back and sides of a violin didn't have a significant influence on the sound made, the sound quality was substantially influenced by the top of the instrument. Norway spruce is an ideal what is called 'tonewood', because although light it is dense so it can be carved very thinly but still remain strong enough to retain its shape and strength even under the high pressure produced from the tensioned strings. Spruce wood is also used to makes a brace (brace bar) which is glued under the table, a sound-post which is located under the bridge and blocks to support the corners. Because of the denseness of the wood these all allow the vibrations of the strings to resonate throughout the body of the instrument.

There are stories of the great violin makers going out into high elevation spruce forests and selecting trees for their instruments by tapping trunks. It's a good story - whether or not it is true we will never know - but as long as members of the violin family of instruments have been made there have undoubtedly been people who have developed skills to identify ideal spruce trees for the purpose. And tone wood experts provide that service for luthiers today.

The most desirable wood comes from trees which are probably 250 or more years old. They are rare, have to be very carefully felled and the tonewood is cut only from the branchless lower part of the trunk. Particularly highly valued is 'moonwood', a name given to wood derived from trees which have been felled when there is a new moon between October and January. This is believed to be when the tree trunk contains less water, which improves the wood's stiffness.

Old wives tale? Maybe. But if you have persevered with reading my scribbles so far maybe you will see the Norway spruce Christmas tree in a new light.

THE ONION

Admit it. When you read the subject of this article you couldn't resist saying *'He must know his onions'*. Then I bet you asked yourself *'Where did the saying come from'*. Relax, I have done the research for you.

The consensus of opinion is that it originated in America during the 'wacky' 1920s when such sayings were rife, one of several phrases implying knowing one's stuff (others were to know one's oats, apples, eggs and even sweet potatoes). First published in the magazine Harper's Bazaar in March 1922, it was, according to one author, *'mildly juvenile wordplay that characterises (an) American linguistic fad of the flapper period'*. No, I don't think you are 'mildly juvenile'.

The wild onion is extinct and because they were small with soft tissues which left no archaeological traces, no-one knows when or where the plant first appeared on planet earth. Ancient records of their use span both eastern and western Asia, so the best guess is that they first appeared in central Asia. It is likely that they were part of the diet of our prehistoric ancestors. Their spread around the world would have been due to their flavour, ability to grow in widely different soils and climates and the fact that they could be dried and preserved for times when food was scarce.

There are records of onions being cultivated in Chinese gardens at least 5000 years ago. They are mentioned in writings in India and Egypt which date back to 3500BC and the Bible tells us that in 1400 BC the Israelites liked onions (Numbers C11:V5 - go, look it up). In ancient Egypt onions were objects of veneration, the circle-within-circle anatomy of the bulb being thought to represent eternal life. Paintings of onions feature on the inner walls of pyramids and tombs. There are depictions of Egyptian priests holding onions and covering an altar with onion leaves and roots. The Egyptian King Ramses IV, who died in 1160BC, was entombed with onions embedded in his eye sockets. Some Egyptologists suggest that the onion was venerated because it was thought that its strong scent and believed magical powers would enable the deceased to breathe again in the afterlife.

In the first century AD there are records of big quantities of onions being eaten, onion juice drunk and onions being rubbed on bodies to fortify athletes for the Olympic Games. The Romans carried onions during their travels to their provinces: writing in Pompeii, before being overcome by the fumes when Vesuvius erupted, Pliny the Elder listed onions as being able to cure vision, induce sleep, heal mouth sores, dog bites, toothaches, dysentery and lumbago. With such perceived attributes it is not surprising that during the post-eruption excavation of Pompeii gardens were found with telltale holes showing where onions had been grown.

By the Middle Ages the three main vegetables used in European cuisine were beans, cabbage and onions. Onions were still considered to have medical qualities, particularly for relieving headaches, curing snake bites and hair loss. They were also used for the payment of rents and as wedding gifts. With such credentials it isn't surprising that the Pilgrims took onions with them on the Mayflower. There are records of onions being planted in 1648 by the Pilgrims as soon as they managed to clear land. It must have come as a surprise to them to discover that wild onions had beaten them to the New World: Native Americans ate them raw or cooked as a seasoning or vegetable, in syrups, as poultices, as an ingredient in dyes and even as toys.

Why do onions make us cry? I found the (probable) answer in an American university paper published in 2017 in which the authors say that it is all to do with the plant's defensive mechanism. Onions grow underground where they are subject to being attacked by countless creatures looking for something to eat. Sulphur in the soil mixes with the growing onion to create sulphoxides. When the outer skin of an onion is broken the sulphoxides and onion enzymes (proteins which speed up chemical reactions) are released. This creates a mild sulphuric acid which reacts with the enzymes to produce a gas which deters the attacking creatures. When we cut into an onion it thinks (I know it doesn't but you know what I mean) that it is being attacked and the chemical process starts. Our eyes react to the gas by producing tears in an attempt to flush it out.

Are 'onion tears' the same as laughing or sad ones? 'Yes', said Charles Darwin. After spending years studying them he came to the conclusion that tears were just a simple device to wet and protect the eyes. But the great man was wrong. We produce three different types of tears: the daily sort, which are constantly secreted and serve to lubricate and protect our eyes when we blink, 'psychic tears' which respond to our emotions (laughter and sadness) and 'reflex tears' which are released in response to irritants like wind, smoke and cut onions. All tears are mixtures of salt water, oils, antibodies and enzymes but the different types of tear have different chemical compositions and look vastly different under a microscope.

The Holy Grail for onion scientists (yes there are some around) is an onion which doesn't irritate the eyes when cut; and after some thirty years research in America they came up with the answer - the 'sunion', claimed to be mild, crunchy and sweet and, most importantly, not to stimulate tears.

If you have to use traditional tear-inducing varieties the sting-ing eyes and consequent tears are said to be reduced by freezing them, soaking them in cold water, keeping a piece of bread in the mouth or wearing goggles. If your eyes are particularly sensitive the only other option is to avoid onions altogether – but then how will you cure your insomnia, toothache, hair loss ----------?

TOBACCO

'*Smoking is a custom loathsome to the eyes, hateful to the nose, harmful to the brain and dangerous to the lungs'.* That total condemnation of tobacco smoking appeared in an anonymous article published in 1604 in a pamphlet with the title *Counterblaste to Tobacco*. Would smoking have become as fashionable as it did in the 17th century if readers had known that the author was no less a person than their monarch, King James 1/ V1? Probably, because the cured leaves of tobacco plants are said to be the third most addictive commonly used drug after heroin and cocaine. They have probably killed more people than any other species of plant on the planet.

The English word *tobacco* comes from the Spanish/ Portuguese word *tabaco*. The botanical name of the plant is *Nicotiana tabacum*; '*Nicotiana*' after the French diplomat Jean Nicot who introduced tobacco to the French court in the 16th century; 'tabacum', possibly from the Caribbean word *tabago,* the name of a y-shaped pipe used by native people for sniffing tobacco smoke.

For botany-loving readers, there are some 75 naturally occurring species of Nicotiana, 49 of which are native to the Americas and 25 to Australia. Through hybridization some 200,000 years ago *N. tabacum* evolved as a distinct species in tropical and subtropical America. There are said to be about 1600 cultivated varieties of this species, but only three are commonly cultivated commercially for the production of smoking tobacco; Virginia, Burley and Oriental, which are all grown under distinct agricultural and curing practices.

When Europeans first arrived in the Americas in 1492 they found that there were long-established tobacco smoking, chewing and snuffing traditions amongst the native people. Amerindians used tobacco and other psychotropic plants in the pursuit of the supernatural, mainly because of their physiological and mind-altering effects. It was also commonly used as a medicine, the crushed leaves being made into poultices to soothe rheumatism and eczema. They were also placed on gums to relieve toothache and chewed leaves were applied to cuts and bound on rattlesnake bites after the poison had been sucked out.

Sir Walter Raleigh is credited with bringing tobacco to England in 1586, but it was being smoked my Spanish and Portuguese sailors long before that: British sailors probably introduced the practice of pipe smoking to England as early as 1565. The decades-long story of the progression of pipe to cigarette smoking, the contested, slow recognition of its harmful effects, appeals of medical bodies, rearguard reactions of the pro-smoking lobby, advert and smoking bans and much else will be well-known to readers. Worldwide the tobacco plant has had a very bad press. I want to balance the plant's image equation just a little (Anti-smokers, don't stop reading).

Tobacco leaves have to be 'cured' before they can be prepared for smoking. Several methods of curing are used, the most frequent being what is called 'flue curing'. With this process freshly picked tobacco leaves are tied to sticks and put into curing barns which have flues conducting hot air through the barns from external fire boxes. This system exposes the green leaves to heat but not smoke. The leaves are left to 'cure' in the barns usually for about a week.

In the 1980s one major international tobacco company, accused by conservationists of using wood derived from the felling of native trees for their tobacco curing practices, decided to commission a study to find out if the criticism was justified. Four of their subsidiary tobacco companies, in Honduras, Argentina, Nigeria and Bangladesh, were selected for the study. During 1990, to determine how much wood was used to produce standard quantities of cured tobacco leaves, on behalf of the tobacco company I did some detailed studies of flue-curing practices in the selected countries The tobacco farms I visited for the studies ranged from small family ones in Nigeria to huge ones owned by 'Tobacco Barons' in Honduras and Argentina. At every farm I visited I was 'helped' by crowds of charming, poor, smiling local people of all ages, from little more than babies to old men and women. Throughout the year tobacco growing and curing was their entire livelihood - there were no other local sources of employment. It had been that way for generations. Their ancestors would have grown and cured the tobacco leaves used to make the millions of cigarettes collected by organizations like the YMCA and Red Cross and given to soldiers in World War 1. Cigarettes, which were a staple of army life then, were said to create a sense of camaraderie, keep men away from hard drink and, according to one general, 'Were more important than bullets for the troops'.

Maybe that doesn't balance the tobacco-image equation but I think that it tips the scales a bit in the plant's favour.

There are no reliable records to suggest that native tobacco plants can be found in the wild today. Google 'tobacco plants' and you are offered pictures of one or more of the commercial varieties of *Nicotiana tabacum*; tidy fields stocked with serried rows of healthy-looking, big-leaved tobacco plants waiting to be harvested. In their native habitat they would have grown in sunny locations to a height of about 2.5 metres before producing clusters of trumpet-shaped, white/pinkish flowers, whilst manufacturing powerful neurotoxins, particularly one that we now call 'nicotine', in their roots and concentrating them in their leaves to deter browsing herbivores.

All they ever aspired to do was to protect themselves. The rest of the plant's dubious history is down to Homo (so-called) sapiens.

THE COCONUT PALM

We hear lots about plants that are endangered, but not much about plants that are dangerous. Poisonous species are obviously dangerous, but the only one I can think of which can kill you instantly – and I mean 'instantly' - is *Cocos nucifera,* the coconut palm. Historical reports about deaths caused by falling coconuts date back to the 1770s and persist. *'Falling coconuts could strike a person on the ground with a force of almost 2,000 pounds.'* (The New York Times 1985);*'Travellers should watch out for coconuts – the killer fruit',* (Boston Herald 2002); a report of coconut trees being removed from beaches in Queensland, Australia, to guard against *'death by coconut'* (Daily Telegraph 2002); 59 year old man killed when a monkey, trained to harvest coconuts from trees, dropped one on his head (Malaysia 2001)

'Falling coconuts kill 150 people worldwide each year', said George Burgess, Director of the International Shark Attack File in 2002.

The '150' figure can be traced back to a research paper with the title *'Injuries Due to Falling Coconuts'* written .in 1984 by Dr.Peter Barss, Professor of Population and Public Health. In the paper he stated that in Papua New Guinea, where he was based, over a period of four years 2.5% of hospital trauma admissions, and two fatalities, were caused by falling coconuts. The figures were un-scientifically prorated by someone to give a figure of 150 deaths annually worldwide, on the assumption that other places where coconut trees grew would suffer a similar rate of deaths.

The debate about the number of people killed or injured by fall-ing coconuts rumbles on, but meanwhile, if you plan to spend some time this summer lounging on a sun-kissed tropical beach, it would seem sensible not to lie under a coconut palm which has clusters of ripe fruits: death or injury from a 1.4kg.falling coconut would take the shine off your holiday. If you <u>are</u> injured by a fall-ing coconut, when you are asked at the hospital what caused the injuries, strictly speaking you shouldn't say that you were hit by a coco-<u>nut</u> because the fruit of a coconut palm isn't a nut; it's a fibrous one-seeded <u>drupe,</u> a fruit with three layers, an outer one, a fleshy middle one and a woody layer that surrounds the seed. But perhaps best to keep that botanical wisdom to yourself until after your wounds have been attended to.

The generic name *Cocos* is thought to be derived from a mid 16th century Spanish/Portuguese word *Coco* meaning 'grinning face', reflecting the fact that a coconut's surface has three germinating pores which look like a smiling face. The specific name *nucifera* is rooted in the Latin words *fero* (I bear) and *nux* (a nut) – hence liter-ally nut-bearing.

Fossil records tell us that wild coconut-like plants evolved some 20 million years ago, long before Homo species appeared on earth. Botanists argue about where they originated, but the money seems to be on Malesia, a botanical region broadly corres-ponding today with the Malay Peninsula, New Guinea, Indonesia and Australia. Initially coconuts dispersed round the world by floating in the sea for months from island to island, the embryonic seeds protected from sea water by the fruit's thick husks. If lucky enough to be washed up on the shore of a coral island and dumped by a wave in a pest and disease free, rooting-friendly habitat, a coconut would germinate, stretching out to the sun light as it grew. The whole process, which can take up to 100 years, is still discretely happening.

The coconut palm must rate as one of mankind's most useful plants. There is evidence of the fruits being used by Bronze Age people living in the Indus Valley, now located in Pakistan and north-west India, as long ago as 3100 -2800BC. The first sight many of us had of a coconut fruit was probably at a fairground coconut shie (from an old English word for 'throw'). It is said that not a cell of the plant went unused. Coconut fibres were made into matting; the white 'kernel', called *copra*, was used to make soap and margarine, dried kernel was fed to babies, and sweets and chutneys were made from ripe kernel, baskets and mats were made from woven leaves and brooms from interwoven stalks, grated kernel was made into creams that lightened floury rice dishes. Many readers will have bored holes in coconuts and sipped the so-called *'milk'* without knowing how special it is. Perfectly sterile, it was the liquid to drink after storms that had polluted the water in wells. It was even used as a sterile intravenous drip for wounded soldiers in World War 2 and the liquid was fermented into a drink which, distilled, turned into the brain-shattering spirit arrack. Many of these practises continue today.

With the coconut palm having served mankind for thousands of years in such diverse ways, I can think of no better way to close this scribble by quoting some of the words from a poem titled *The Coconut*, written by the American poet Frederick Seidel (born 1936):

A coconut can fall and hit you on the head,
And if it falls from high enough can kind of knock you dead.
Dead beneath the coconut palms, that's the life for me!
And green jungle and white beaches and the blue South China Sea.

55

BAMBOOS

During a working visit to Bangladesh, whilst wandering around the streets of Dhaka I saw a large house being built. I watched in awe as workers bounced cement-filled wheelbarrows along narrow planks supported by long scaffold poles which, tied by rope, raked the sky at anything but 90 degree angles. It seemed to me to be an accident waiting to happen. I needn't have worried; the workers knew exactly what they were doing. The scaffold poles were made from bamboo which has a higher specific compressive strength than wood, brick or concrete and a specific tensile strength that rivals steel'

.Bamboos are members of the grass family of plants (*Poaceae*; *póa* from the ancient Greek word for fodder). There are some 115 distinct genera and 1400 species which are unevenly distributed throughout tropical, sub-tropical and warm temperate regions of the world. Some species of what are called 'running bamboos' throw up hollow, sectioned culms (stems) from prolific rootstocks which grow rapidly, suppress competing vegetation and develop into impenetrable natural barriers, 'impenetrable' because they not only grow close together but also because the culms are heavily impregnated with silica which quickly dulls even the sharpest of cutting tools.

Together with rice bamboos have played an enormously important role in the development of China and the East. A unique combination of qualities - including lightness, hollowness, flexibility and strength - has resulted in them providing the raw material for hugely diverse purposes. If I listed all the different uses I have discovered it would take up the rest of my permitted word count, so I will just mention a few that most surprised me. Needles for record players, bamboo ash as a jewellery polish and in the manufacture of batteries; electric light filaments, bicycles, exterior cladding on aeroplanes, poison, food, medicine for asthmatics, beer, umbrellas (this is getting tedious - if you want more I'll leave it to you: might make a good party game).

For at least 2500 years bamboo has served mankind both practically and culturally. Confucius (551-479BC) wrote 'People become thin without meat. But without bamboo they become vulgar'. Scholars often planted bamboo in their courtyards and included the Chinese character for bamboo (zhu) in their nicknames. The plant was often equated in poetry and prose with expressions of virtue and morality. The Chinese poet Bai Juyi (772-846AD) defined the model behaviour of a gentleman as being upright as the bamboo, equally as strong and, just as the bamboo culm is hollow, he should keep his mind open and never entertain prejudice or secret thoughts. That's not a bad code for life is it? Maybe a bit of bamboo in our pocket would be a good daily reminder.

The name 'bamboo' *is* derived from an ancient Indian language word *bambu,* which is supposed to sound like the noise it makes when it is being burnt. Botanically they are remarkable. Some species can grow up to 30 metres tall with culms 30 centimetres thick. The family includes the fastest growing plants in the world with some species growing 91cms (3 feet for old-timers) in 24 hours: that's nearly 4cms an hour or 1mm every 90 seconds. If you concentrated you could probably actually watch a plant growing.

Bamboos flower erratically - some species at very long intervals. – then die. The record is held by the Chinese Mainland Bamboo (*Phyllostachys bambusoides*) which can grow 22 metres tall. In the late 1960s it burst into flower at the same time all over the world, produced seeds then promptly died. It wasn't the first time it had happened: Chinese scholars had recorded the species flowering in 999 AD and again in 1114 AD, and after the species had been imported to Japan there were records of it flowering in the early 1700s then next between 1844 and 1847. So, based on an average 120 year cycle, it was due to flower next in the 1960s. Sadly, if you missed it, you are unlikely to see it flowering again.

I know; you expect me to tell you why – and I wish I could. I did try. There have been several explanations over the years, the most recent, and plausible, involving mathematics. I found an erudite paper on the subject and, after struggling to understand it I was bamboozled* so couldn't summarize it in a few words. Suffice it to say that the hypothesis involves 'predator satiation', 'stabilizing selection' and 'integermultiplication'. Still interested? It's all there on the web: or you can just close your eyes and be fascinated by yet another of Mother Nature's miracles.

They are so closely associated that I must mention the giant panda, for which, although dentally carnivorous, bamboo makes up some 99% of its diet They favour some 20 species of bamboo, preferring in the spring to munch shoots, which are rich in nitrogen and phosphorus but lack calcium, and leaves, which have a higher calcium content, in summer. As bamboo has very little nutritional value, giant pandas must eat up to 40kg. of the plant every day. Research suggests that some 7 million years ago environmental changes killed off most of giant pandas' prey so only those which managed to adapt and become more vegetarian survived. Gradually this made them lose their taste for meat and 2 million years ago they had evolved to become bamboo eaters.

Life's tough for giant pandas in the wild. Records from the Quin

Mountains in China showed that over a period of 37 years, 25 giant pandas died or became ill during spring following the hardships of winter. And they must suffer from toothache as the high silica content in bamboo damages their teeth.

Perhaps, when things get tough, we should say it's a panda's rather than a dog's life.

*bamboozle: sadly, for me, the word has nothing to do with bamboo, possibly coming from the French *'embabouiner'* to make a fool (literally 'baboon') of someone

POPPIES

Papaver somniferum

If any plant can be called enigmatic it must be the opium poppy for it has been both a blessing and curse to mankind. Native to a region that ranges from Turkey, East to Afghanistan, India, Myanmar and Thailand, for centuries the disarmingly pretty plant decorated gardens of the wealthy and was used as part of floral decorations. *Papaver somniferum* (*'Papaver'* the Latin name for a poppy; *'somniferum'* after Somnus the Roman god of sleep) grows quickly up to a height of one metre. As a 'blessing' it is the source of the healing balm morphine; as a 'curse' one of its derivatives, heroin, has had catastrophic effects on mankind worldwide – and (correct me if I'm wrong) it has the unenviable reputation of being the only plant to have caused a war..

Said to have been exploited by man (alright – and women) for at least 6000 years, the earliest reference to the plant being cultivated is in 3400 BC in Southwest Asia where the Sumerian people called it *Hul Gil,* the 'joy plant'. With such a reputation it isn't surprising that people began to cultivate it to increase its availability and reduce its cost, and it soon found its way along the Silk Road, West to the Mediterranean and East to China.

For centuries what was commonly called 'Milk of the poppy' (now called 'opium'), was prescribed for almost every ailment. The name aptly describes the milk-like latex found in the capsules enclosing the seeds of the plant from which, when dried, morphine, codeine and heroin are derived. The name 'opium' comes from the ancient Greeks name for the sap – 'opion'.

My quest to find out how and why *Papaver somniferum* got its pain-relieving properties led me down a lot of blind alleys until I discovered that a team of researchers has been studying the subject for several years. Unsurprisingly their findings are abstruse and difficult to summarise briefly – but here goes.

By chance, over millions of years, the genetic composition of *Papaver somniferum* plants underwent major changes (boffins call them 'mutations'). One or more of these mutations created a gene which produces an enzyme that converts poppy molecules into compounds that eventually become morphine and codeine. Without that gene *Papaver somniferum* wouldn't have pain-killing properties: there are many varieties of the species that have little or none. That's the much-simplified answer to 'how'. Charles Darwin and his 'Survival of the Fittest' theory probably provide the answer to 'why'. Herbivorous animals, sleeping or dozy after munching poppy plants, are more vulnerable than alert animals to carnivorous predators. So natural selection will favour animals that don't browse on poppy plants. By chance the plants have evolved a defence system against browsing herbivores. And it will still be evolving. (It's not scientific to call it clever).

In 1805 Friedrich Sertürner discovered morphine whilst working as an assistant in a pharmacy in Germany. He named the substance he had isolated 'morphine' after Morpheus, the ancient Greek god of sleep and dreams, and to prove that it was the active ingredient in opium he publically experimented on himself and three friends. When convinced, physicians called it 'God's own medicine' because of its reliability, long-lasting effects and safety. Ironically, in a quest to find a non-addictive alternative to morphine, Charles Wright, a chemistry lecturer in London, isolated the seriously addictive substance diamorphine in 1874. In 1898 the German pharmaceutical company Bayer began manufacturing it as a non-addictive pain medication under the brand name 'heroin' (possibly derived from the ancient Greek word for a hero: people who took the drug said they felt heroic). When its addictive potential was recognized the drug's production was stopped in 1913. The rest of the sad heroin story and record is history.

With demand increasing in Britain for Chinese porcelain, silk and particularly tea, and reluctance of the Chinese Manchu leaders to trade with the west, in the early 1800s British traders cynically introduced opium into China from British-owned Bengal. They weren't the first to; Turkish and Arab traders had introduced the drug into China in the late 1500s. Until the 17th century it had been used in relatively small quantities to relieve pain. Then tobacco began to be imported into China and pipe smoking became popular. By 1729 opium smoking had become such a problem that the emperor prohibited its import and smoking. Despite the decree the opium trade continued to flourish. By 1773 the British had discovered how profitable the trade was and became the leading supplier of opium into China. By 1793 the British East India Company had established a monopoly on the opium trade and poppy growers in India were forbidden to sell to competitors.

The rest of the story is far too long and complicated to even briefly summarize in a short article (it's not an easy read). Suffice it to say that soaring opium addiction rates in China led to two so-called 'Opium Wars' in the mid 19th century, both of which China lost, forcing the opening of Chinese ports to western traders and the giving of Hong Kong to Britain. Opium imports continued to increase after the wars and unsurprisingly, with the predominantly peasant farmer population largely debilitated by famine and opium addiction, this led to a revolution. Privately owned land was seized by the people and given to communities; Mao Zedong rose to become Communist leader in 1949 and instigated the so-called 'Cultural Revolution' from 1966 until his death in 1976. According to some commentators the revolution paralysed China politically, damaged the economy and society and caused the death of possibly as many as two million people.

William Gladstone (British Prime Minister 1892 to 1894) wrote in his diary, "I am in dread of the judgements of God upon England for our national iniquity towards China". An 'iniquity' substantially influenced by *Papaver somniforum.*

The Common Poppy Field Or Shirley Poppy

Monet and Van Gogh couldn't resist painting them and poets have waxed lyrical over them so it would be remiss of me not to give some space to one of the opium poppy's cousins - *Papaver rhoeas* ('*Papaver*' you already know; '*rhoeas*' the Greek word for red). It goes by many names - common, field and Shirley poppy, corn rose, red weal and others – but we know it best as the Flanders poppy because, growing from seeds that can remain dormant in the soil for a hundred years, they were the first flowers to appear in the blitzed ground of the Flanders region of Belgium in World War 1.

Papaver rheos

Within living memory, until the arrival of selective herbicides, blood red poppies adorned Britain's farmland during the summer months, frustrating farmers by reducing the productivity of agricultural crops. Having long been associated with mankind it is not surprising that it has established a firm place in folklore. It was called the Thunder-flower and children were told that if a petal fell off the flower when it was picked the gatherer could be struck by lightning (Northumberland 1853). If a flower was held too near an eye it would cause blindness (Yorkshire 1886), too near an ear would cause violent earache (Nottinghamshire 1878) and if smelled nosebleeds would follow that could only be stopped by pushing a spider's cobweb up the nostrils (Cambridgeshire 1952). All nonsense? Perhaps – but not without purpose. The pretty red flowers must have tempted children to wade through farm crops to pick them. The prospect of being struck by lightning, becoming blind, having nosebleeds or earache would have been good deterrents.

On 2nd May 1915 during the bloody second battle of Ypres, twenty-two year old Lieutenant Alexis Heimer was killed by an enemy shell. His death was witnessed by a close friend, forty-two year old Canadian Major John McCrea who, with no chaplain available, the next morning performed funeral rites over those parts of his friend's body that could be recovered. The stories of what followed are many and varied, but there is no doubt that McCrea was so moved by his friend's death that, soon after the burial, motivated by the simple wooden crosses and clusters of field poppies that marked the improvised graveyard, he scribbled a poem in a notebook, starting with –

> *In Flanders Fields the poppies blow*
> *Between the crosses, row on row.*
> *That mark the place; and in the sky*
> *The larks, still bravely singing, fly*
> *Scarce heard amid the guns below.*

The three stanza poem was saved from being lost to posterity by a fellow officer who stopped McCrae from destroying it. McCrae eventually sent it to *Punch* magazine where, during December 1915, it was published in the bottom corner of an inside page with no attribution. Sadly John McCrea didn't survive the war, dying from pneumonia during January 1918. He was never to know what a profound influence his words would have on posterity. .

The story travels now to the city of New York where, on 9th November 1918, two days before the Armistice was declared forty-seven year old Professor Moina Michael was attending a YMCA Conference. On her desk lay a copy of the American *Ladies Home Journal.* Browsing through it she came across a copy of McCrae's poem. It wasn't the first time that she had seen it but this time the words had such a profound effect on her that she picked up a yellow envelope and on a blank side scribbled her own verse starting with -

> *We cherish, too, the poppy red*
> *That grows on fields where valor led.*

She gave it the title 'We Shall Keep The Faith' and pledged that from that moment she would always to wear a red poppy.

Fired by her commitment that afternoon Moina scoured the

local shops until she found one large and twenty four small, silk poppies resembling the wild poppies of Flanders. Her story had got around the conference's male delegates who were so impressed that when they saw her wearing one pinned on her coat, during the evening asked her if she had any more. The remaining twenty-four poppies were duly distributed around the group: it was the first occasion when poppies were worn in memory of soldiers who had died in battle.

Moina's tireless campaign over the following years to make the poppy a national remembrance symbol, at her own expense, earned her the title 'The Poppy Lady', and the money raised every year from the sale of Remembrance Day poppies continues to help veterans from all wars and their families.

THE POTATO

The poppy had a profound effect on the history of China, but a small tuber native to South America, had an even bigger influence on the fate of one country (Ireland) and the population of another (the United States of America).

Google 'Irish potato famine' and you will find that the web is awash with sickening photographs of abjectly poor people being evicted from humble cottages, homesteads being bulldozed and starving families, carrying a few meagre possessions, plodding away from burning dwellings. (Skip the next bit if it's depressing you). Some found their way to the slums of Dublin, Cork and Belfast. Figures vary but between 1845 and 1850, as a direct result of the potato famine, in Ireland an estimated one million people died and an additional one million emigrated, many in what were called 'coffin ships', to North America, Australia and New Zealand. Between 1841 and 1851 the population of Ireland fell from 8 million to 6.5 million: today some 32 million people living in the USA (10% of the population) claim Irish ancestry.

Potato plants are believed to have originated 13000 years ago in an area now part of south Peru and northeast Bolivia, then slowly spread north to the south of the United States and south to southern Chile in which area some 180 species are now considered to be native. Scientists think that it began to be cultivated by indigenous people between 3000 and 7000 years ago; depictions of potatoes have been found on pottery in Peru dated back to pre-Incan civilizations. The commercial potatoes we consume in vast quantities today derive from the wild species *Solanum tuberosum,* the generic name, *'Solanum',* possibly derived from the Latin word for sun, *sol,* indicating the plant's affinity for sunlight and the specific name *'tuberosum',* referring to the swollen roots or 'tubers', from the Latin *tuber* for a lump.

The Spanish conquistadors were probably the first Europeans to encounter potatoes when they arrived in Peru in 1532 and saw Inca miners eating chuñu, made from dried potatoes (There are recipes for it on the web, but don't rush).. Although they used potatoes as part of their basic ship rations, with their minds focussed on their search for gold and silver, the Spaniards didn't recognize the plant's enormous potential value. But they did like the pretty potato plant flowers, so, probably in 1570, they began to take plants back to Spain. It didn't take long before a few Spanish farmers began to cultivate the plants and use the tubers to make food for livestock. By 1600 potato plants had spread throughout much of Europe where they were grown mainly as attractive novelty plants in gardens. As food they were regarded with suspicion, distaste and fear, considered unfit for human consumption and used only for animal feed. Unless starving even peasants ate them only as a last resort, partly because of the plants resemblance to the poisonous nightshade family (same family) and the latter's association with witches and devils.

The potato probably arrived in England in 1586, brought by colonists returning from Virginia where they were sent by Sir Walter Raleigh. In a report written by Thomas Harriot, a mathematician and astronomer (1560-1621), he called the plant 'openank' (don't ask me: any information on the etymology will be welcome) and described it as having 'roots as large as a walnut and others much larger (that) grow together in damp soil and are good food either boiled or roasted'. The Nantwich botanist John Gerarde was the first person to catalogue the potato. In his 1597 "Herbal" he called it the "Potato of Virginia", from the Spanish *patata,* derived from the Haitian word *batata* which originally referred to, but eventually became distinct from, what we now call the sweet potato.

Sir Walter Raleigh is said to have been the first person to grow potatoes in the British Isles when he planted them at his estate near C33ork in Ireland. By 1597 they were being grown in Gerarde's garden in Lancashire where they were considered to be a delicate dish, roasted, steeped in sugar, wine, baked with marrow and spices or even preserved and candied. Although the so-called 'upper classes' may have seen the food potential of potatoes they were not popular with the superstitious 'lower classes'. Gardening books in the late 1600s described them as "food for poor people", "much used for bread in Ireland and America" and "food for swine or cattle".

But their popularity and excellent qualities slowly spread and by the mid 1700s they were well known and widely cultivated. Today potatoes are grown in more than one hundred countries and rank as the world's third most important food crop after rice and wheat.

Finally, because I am sure some readers will want to know why they peel 'spuds', I thought you would feel short-changed if I didn't try to find out where the name 'spud' came from. The origin of the word itself seems unknown, but the first documented reference to it occurs in New Zealand in 1875 when it was described as a sharp, narrow spade used to dig up large-rooted plants. Commonly used to dig up potatoes, in time the name was adopted as the nickname for the potato itself and as such spread round the English-speaking world. The rest, as they say, is history

FERNS

Anthropologists tell us that our ancestry goes back some 4 million years when human evolution branched away from that of other primates. That's a very long time ago, but nothing when compared with the evolutionary history of ferns. They first appeared on planet earth 350 million years ago, during what we now call the Carboniferous period, and dominated much of the supercontinent we call Pangaea (from Ancient Greek *'pan'* meaning entire and *'Gaia'* meaning earth).

Long before dinosaurs roamed the earth primitive, and many huge, amphibians and reptiles crawled through flat swampy land populated by an extensive and luxuriant vegetation, including 20 metre tall ancestors of horsetails and 9 metre tall ancestors of ferns, destined to becoming partly responsible for the problems and worries we have today with global warming and climate change.

Warmed by the sun's rays, the fern's 'fronds' - the name given to the long, feathery leaves of ferns and palms - soaked up carbon dioxide from the atmosphere until they either fell and were eaten, turned into compost or buried in swampy sediment. Over millions of years what was initially spongy peat was compressed into carbon-rich strata packed with latent energy. You've got it; the once lauded but now problematic 'coal'.

Probably because our early ancestors found it easier to burn wood that grew on the surface than coal that had to be dug up, it took a long time before they began to make serious use of coal, although one Bronze Age tribe living in Wales is believed to have used it to fire funeral pyres. After they discovered the delights of northern Europe, and decided to stay, the Romans used coal to heat their hot baths and under-floor heating systems, but after they left Britain in 410CE coal seems to have been little used for some 1100 years until medieval times when it was being traded by monasteries in County Durham. By the 1700s coal trading had become big business. The rest of the coal story has been well-versed over the years, but it is relatively recently that the reputation of what was once called 'black gold' has been severely tarnished by it being linked with asthma, cancer, heart and lung ailments, acid rain, global warming and most of the world's environmental problems.

Botanists tell us that there are some 12,000 species of ferns growing all around the world in a variety of habitats and in forms including trees, vines and shrub-like plants. To enable them to reproduce away from water - remember, their early ancestors lived in swamps - they have evolved a two-stage way to reproduce. Look on the underside of a mature fern frond and you will probably see rows or clusters of brown dots called *sori* (from the Greek *sōros* meaning 'heap': 'probably' because not every frond has them). Each sorus contains *sporangia* (from the Greek *spora* 'spore' and *angeion* 'vessel'). When mature the sporangia burst open, propelling clouds of minute spores away from the parent plant. If a spore lands on a suitable site – fortunately most don't or are eaten by insects otherwise the earth would be covered with ferns - it produces a small flat green *prothallus* (from the

Latin *pro* 'before' and Greek *thallos* 'green shoot'), attached to the soil by simple roots. Each prothallus contains male and female sexual organs (nothing explicit follows) that self-fertilize. Some six months later, from the underside of the prothallus a new fern begins to slowly unroll – resembling violin scrolls they are called *fiddleheads* – that grow into a new fern plant to start the cycle over again. Fascinating, isn't it?

Fern 'fiddleheads

With ferns having existed on earth long before the earliest hominids it's not surprising that they became part of our ancestors' folklore. Gathering, or even touching, fern fronds were thought to invite bad luck in Staffordshire in 1862. Conversely bunches of fern fronds were kept in some houses because it was thought that they provided protection from thunder, lightning and storms. According to a Welsh superstition it was dangerous to carry fern fronds because they attracted adders, yet as recently as 1909 some Welsh waggoners would put a bunch of fern fronds over a horse's ears to 'keep the devil away' and 'baffle witches' *(Folklore of Wales 1989).* Cutting or burning bracken, a genus of large, coarse ferns, was believed to cause rain. In 1636, prior to a visit by Charles I to Staffordshire, his Chamberlain wrote to the High Sherriff of the county and asked him to order that no ferns were burnt during the king's visit, to ensure fine weather.

Perhaps the strangest fern-related superstition was the belief that the spores, called fernseed, made people invisible. It's difficult to understand how such an unlikely, easily tested, belief could have arisen, but it did. Shakespeare mentions it in *Henry the Fourth Part 2* (*'We have the receipt of Fernseed, we walke invisible'*). The belief, which persisted in parts of Britain until at least the end of the 19th century, derived from the idea that as nobody had seen fern seeds they must be invisible, so when you found some they would make you invisible too. But how do you collect 'invisible' seeds? It took a lot of research but I found the answer. Around midnight on mid-summer eve the seeds become visible for a few moments as they fall to the ground. Catch them on a pewter plate and you will be invisible.

I hope that helps

TEA

Life without a cuppa! It's inconceivable, isn't it? But it wasn't for most of our ancestors who had never heard of a drink made from the dried leaves of *Camellia sinensis* (generic name *'Camelia'*, given by Linnaeus after the Moravian botanist Joseph Kamel (1661–1706); specific name *'sinensis'* a Latin word meaning 'from China'). When it began to appear in London coffee houses in 1657 it couldn't have been very popular because one coffee house owner felt it necessary to explain in an advert that the new beverage was an *"Excellent, and by all Physicians approved, China drink, called by the Chinese, Tcha'*. A year later 'tee' was being sold in many of the London coffee houses and, growing in popularity, it became a drink for the wealthy and fashionable set. After sampling it in 1660 the diarist Samuel Pepys, always willing to try something new, wrote in his diary, *'I did send for a cup of tee, (a China drink) of which I never had drunk before'*.

Camellia sinensis is a small tree which is native to an area which stretches from India to China. The leaves and shoots have been used to make a drink for at least 4500 years: legend says that the drink was first discovered by the Chinese emperor Shen Nung in 2737 BC when some leaves blew into hot water (that takes a bit of swallowing). The beverage was certainly known in the time of the Chinese polymath Confucius (551–479 BC), and by the seventh century AD it had become the national drink of China.

The Dutch were probably the first Europeans to drink tea after their merchant traders brought the leaves from China to Holland in 1610, but it took many years for the drink to become really popular in Britain. For that we have to thank Portuguese Catherine of Braganza, who married King Charles II in 1662. Her infectious enthusiasm for the drink spread through the court and country, making it popular with the bourgeoisie. During the 18th and 19th centuries Europeans generally turned their backs on traditional drinks like small beers, cheap ale and often polluted well water and began to drink more tea. – and the more they drank the more they wanted because, like coffee, tea contains the stimulant caffeine.

But it wasn't universally popular. The journalist, farmer and Member of Parliament William Cobbett (1763-1835) wrote in 1821, *'It is, in fact, a weaker kind of laudanum which enlivens for the moment and weakens thereafter'*. His words had little effect; tea consumption, by rich and poor, grew and the rest is history. Despite a reported recent decline in tea drinking, we Brits still consume on average about 3 cups per person every day, making us one of the highest per capita consumers of tea in the world, beaten only by Turkey and Eire.

It may sound unlikely but *Camellia sinensis* influenced the design of ships. Until the 1850s long-haul cargo-carrying ships were heavy, lumbering vessels built from as much as 1000 tons of seasoned oak. The collapse of the East India Company in 1833 opened up international competition in the tea trade. British and American traders began to build sleek, faster-sailing 'clippers' – so-named because they *'clipped'* across the seas – with sharp bows that could cut through the waves. With fair winds the aerodynamically-designed ships achieved hitherto unheard of speeds: the *Sovereign of the Seas* achieved the highest speed recorded of 22 knots (25 mph) in 1854 whilst sailing to Australia. Conveniently ignoring the fact that fresh tea tastes no different from tea that has been kept for a year in a warehouse, tea traders made the most of the widely publicised races of famous clipper captains as they battled the weather to be the first of a season's cargo of tea back to London from China.

Although tea has only been known in Britain for 350 years tea traditions and superstitions were well established by the 19th century and some persist even today. If water is put into a teapot and the tea forgotten it is a sign of impending misfortune (*Trowbridge 1923*). If you unwittingly make tea weaker than intended a friend is turning away from you (*Ipswich 1953*). Stirring someone else's tea will stir up trouble (*Sudbury 1975*). It is considered bad luck for two people, especially women, to pour tea from the same pot (*Kent 1983*). Spilling a spoonful of tea when you are making a brew is a lucky omen for the mother of the house (*Taunton 1985*).

Last but by no means least, *Camellia sinensis* adopted tasseography (from *tasse*, the French word for a cup) – divining the future by interpreting patterns in tea leaves. 'Adopted' because the practice didn't begin with tea leaves – it is said to go back to medieval fortune tellers who fabricated readings for gullible clients from wax, lead or other molten substances. With the arrival of tea, enterprising fortune tellers simply adapted a long-established practice to residues of the new drink

THE CINCHONA TREE

If you start with 'Once upon a time', it makes a lovely bedtime story.

In the year 1638, in the country we now call Peru, the beautiful young wife of the Viceroy, the Count of Chinchon, lay on her bed dying from malaria. Traditional 'cures' had been tried to no effect and the distraught count asked the court physician if there was any other cure that could be tried. Nervously, the doctor said that he had heard of a possible remedy used by some native tribes to cure shivering sickness – a drink called quinquina, made from dissolving the powdered bark of some native trees in water. The count ordered men to be sent immediately to obtain some of the bark, which was easier said than done as the nearest source was some 500 miles north in modern Equador. The bark was obtained and after being given the elixir the countess was cured. You can end with 'And they all lived happily ever after'.

That isn't the end of the story. The countess is also said to have taken some of the bark with her on her return to Europe in the 1640s and used it to treat people suffering from malaria due to living in the mosquito-infested wetlands surrounding her husband's estate at Chinchon, about 25 miles southeast of Madrid. In memory of the story, in 1742 Linnaeus named the genus of the trees from which the bark is obtained, *Cinchona,* unwittingly omitting the 'h'.

The story is claimed to be important because the countess was the first European on record to have been cured by quinine, an alkaloid in the bark of some native South American trees.

Readers of my scribbles will know that I try to avoid short-changing them, so I decided to do some research to see if the story is true.

'No', says Thomas Gale in encyclopedia.com. The countess never had malaria and died in Colombia before returning to Spain.

Another record about the discovery of quinine says that in the early 1600s Spanish colonists in Peru noticed the native Quechua people adding water to the ground up bark of trees and drinking it to relieve shivering due to fevers. The native's 'fevers' probably weren't due to malaria, which wasn't endemic in the Americas, but long before the countess was given a bark-based elixir, Spaniards had tried similar potions to treat the disease which they had brought with them from Europe after 1492.

But Dr.Juliet Burba of Minnesota University is not so sure. In a paper on the subject of malaria and quinine, she quotes Antonio de Calancha, a monk, who, in an article published in 1630 on the Augustine Order, made a brief reference to the forests of the Andes Mountains in which he said '*A tree grows which they call the fever tree in the county of Loxa, whose bark, of the colour of cinnamon, made into powder amounting to the weight of two small coins and given in a beverage, cures the fevers'.* Dr. Burba says that historians' debate whether or not the bark of what came to be called 'cinchona trees' was a medicine used by indigenous people or was discovered by European colonists. She believes that native people probably didn't know about the medicinal value of cinchona bark, no mention of which appears in early Inca pharmacopoeias.

So, as Aldous Huxley said, it seems to be another case of 'You pays your money and you takes your choice,

The name 'quinine' is said to derive from a native name for cinchona trees, '*Quina-Quina*' or '*Quinquina*'. The true story of its discovery may never be known, but one thing is certain – mankind owes a great debt of gratitude to cinchona trees. Evergreen, and growing up to a height of 30 metres, there are at least 23 species, some better than others in terms of their medicinal value, but all native to the slopes of the Andean Mountains.

When they realized the bark's medicinal value the Spaniards developed an industry around cinchona trees. It was enormously profitable. Bark, harvested from trees, was taken to Paita, a coastal city in north-western Peru, where it was loaded onto ships, taken to Panama and eventually transported via Havana to Spain. The initial scepticism or many European doctors about the medicinal value of what came to be called 'Jesuit's Bark' was allayed when it was seen to have cured huge numbers of people from 'ague', including Kings Charles 11 of England and Louis XIV of France. Cinchona bark/quinine had a major influence on the history of mankind. By enabling people to survive in malaria-ridden parts of Africa and Asia it encouraged colonization by Europeans. For decades the Spanish managed to monopolize the cinchona industry but eventually British and Dutch explorers smuggled seeds and saplings out of South America and started plantations in Europe and other parts of the world.

We also have to thank cinchona trees for something that is part of British culture. Quinine tastes bitter so, in the early 19th century, British colonials in India hit on the idea of mixing their daily dose of quinine water with gin and lime to make it more palatable: so our popular G&T drink was born.

I'll finish with another story – one that illustrates the folly of bigotry.

In 1658 'Lord Protector' Oliver Cromwell was dying from malaria. He refused to take the 'Peruvian' or 'Jesuit's' bark because it was a 'Popish remedy' – and died.

True or anecdotal? I don't know. But I'm writing this on a Sunday so I'll call it The Parable of the Cinchona Tree.

THE MISTLETOE

Growing, bush-like and seemingly rootless, high in the crowns of big trees, mistletoe has been revered by mankind for millennia.

In his book *Natural History,* written in AD77, the Roman naturalist and philosopher Pliny (23 to 79AD) said that in Gaul, Celtic Druids considered nothing to be more sacred than mistletoe. They believed it provided protection from fire, made farm animals and women fertile, was an antidote to poison and cured epilepsy. It was considered to be particularly sacred if it grew on an oak tree (which it rarely does). When they found some growing on an oak tree, a priest, arrayed in white vestments, climbed the tree and ceremonially removed it on the 6th day after a new moon using a golden sickle, preventing it from falling to the ground by catching it in a white cloak. Don't ask me why it had to be done on the 6th day - experts on the Druids are still arguing about that. And they don't seem to have wondered how a sickle made of gold could be sharpened enough to cut a woody mistletoe stem. It is because of its past association with a pagan culture that it is traditionally banned from churches. In December 1958 the Revd. Joyce banned it from St. Thomas's Church, Derby. When asked why by a *Daily Mirror* journalist he said, 'I have nothing against mistletoe in the home – I enjoy kissing pretty girls under it as much as anyone else – but it has strong connections with the pagan leaders of the Ancient Britons'.

Probably because Ancient Britons adopted many Celtic beliefs, the plant's reputation persisted over the centuries. In his book *Complete Herbal,* written in 1653, Culpepper credits it with the ability to cure a long list of ailments and said 'Some have so highly esteemed it for the virtues thereof, that they have called it *Lignum Sanctiœ Crucis* (Wood of the Holy Cross)'.

Holly and ivy are mentioned as being part of Christmas folk-lore in the Middle Ages, but mistletoe doesn't feature until 1648 when, in his poem *Ceremonies for Candlemas Eve,* Robert Herwick (1591-1674) wrote:

> *Down with the rosemary and bays,*
> *Down with the mistletoe;*
> *Instead of holly, now up-raise*
> *The greener box, for show.*

The plant became a valued part of the kissing-bough tradition in the 18th century when mistletoe branches were hung up in farmhouses and kitchens and rules dictated when they should be taken down. The counties of Warwickshire and Staffordshire were (and possibly still are) exceptions because there mistletoe was supposed to be left up for an entire year to protect the house from lightning and fire.

There are said to be some 1300 species of mistletoe worldwide, some 20 of which are endangered. Mistletoes are mostly semi-parasites, using their leaves, like the majority of plants, to produce some of the food they need by photosynthesis and taking minerals and water from the host tree but seldom killing it. The species found in Britain has the botanical name *Viscum album,*

'*Viscum*' from the Latin *visco,* meaning sticky; '*album*' the Latin for white. Plants, all parts of which are poisonous, are either male or female ('*dioecious*' if you want to impress): the female plants have the white berries. It is spread by birds which feed on the waxy berries that enclose seeds covered in a sticky substance called *viscin.* The birds wipe off some of the sticky seeds on the underside of tree branches: more seeds remain sticky after passing through the bird's digestive system and are deposited on branches where they produce a specially adapted root, called a *haustorium* (from the Latin word *haustus* meaning absorption) that penetrates the bark. The Victorians believed that mistletoe seeds would only germinate if they had passed through the gut of a 'mistle thrush', hence the bird's name today.

The plant came to be called 'mistletoe' because our Ancient Anglo-Saxon ancestors noticed that it often grew where birds left droppings. The Anglo-Saxon word *mistel* means 'dung' and *tan* means 'twig'. Put them together and you have 'dung-on-a twig': a splendidly literal name, but perhaps not one to ask a girl for a kiss under.

Although reluctant to, I feel that I shouldn't finish without commenting on what arguably might be the most important influence that mistletoe has had on mankind, namely its perceived ability to combat cancer. I am 'reluctant' to because; from the numerous academic papers and general articles that have been written about the subject it seems to be a minefield. The theory dates back to the 1920s when the Austrian philosopher Rudolf Steiner (1861–1925) suggested (forgive me, protagonists, for the following grossly simplified summary) that mistletoe might provide a cure for cancer after noticing that the plant survives by sucking nutrients from trees, eventually killing the host (which it seldom does). His theory was that in the same way extracts from the plant might suck out cancerous cells. Although implausible some 1000 in vitro studies have shown that extracts from mistletoe do have anticancer characteristics. A glance at websites will show that today there are many claimed mistletoe/cancer remedies, some treatments even available from the National Health Service. Conversely some medical specialists say that the most reliable controlled trials fail to show benefits and some may even cause harm.

It's another example of 'you pays your money and you takes your choice'.

ABOUT THE AUTHOR

Martyn Baguley

After graduating in Forestry and Applied Botany from the University of Wales, Martyn's long working life as a professional forester took him all over the United Kingdom and to some twenty other countries worldwide.

Starting in 1995 he developed his long-held interest in writing and produced some 350 articles and short stories that were published mainly in national and regional magazines in the United Kingdom and the Republic of Ireland.

With his lifelong interest in the countryside and natural world it is not surprising that many of the articles he has written have been related to these subjects.

PRAISE FOR AUTHOR

BOOKS BY THIS AUTHOR

Wildwood Legacy What Our Native Trees Did For Us

- tells the stories of many of Britain's native trees and the folklore associated with them

Plant Intelligence: Fact Or Fiction?

- the product of a considerable amount of research of academic and general publications, the book introduces readers to the hitherto secret, fascinating parallel world of plants.

Heads And Tales. Stories About Ten Men Who Made A Difference.

- a compilation of articles about ten exceptional men, what they did to achieve fame, the times in which they lived and less well known aspects of their personalities.

www.ingramcontent.com/pod-product-compliance
Lightning Source LLC
Chambersburg PA
CBHW050740260726
48661CB00001B/327